THE UNCONSCIOUS KID

THE UNCONSCIOUS KID

From the playing fields to the drug dens

Paul Hannaford

www.paulhannaford.com
Twitter: @paulhannaford
Instagram: paulhannaford

978-1-8382467-0-9 Paperback
978-1-8382467-1-6 Hardback
978-1-8382467-2-3 Ebook

First hardback and paperback editions, 2020

Front cover photo by Peter Spicer
Copy-editing services by www.bookeditingservices.co.uk
Text design by Richard Marston
Cover design by Jordan Chavoush

Printed and bound by Book Printing UK

DISCLAIMER

The events and conversations in this book have been set down to the best of the author's ability, although some names and details have been changed to protect the privacy of individuals.

A DAY IN THE DRUG DEN

The first thing I feel is pain. Before I even have a thought in my head, or open my eyes, I can feel the pain in my body. It's coming from my throbbing legs. It feels as though someone is trying to amputate them without anaesthetic – raw, naked, undiluted waves of excruciating, nauseating agony. It fills my whole body and my mind. I want to scream. I can't escape it.

The second thing I sense is the smell. Overpowering, rank, both sweet and sour at the same time. Like finding a bag of rotting meat that's been abandoned for days in the sun. It makes me gag. It's coming from the putrid flesh on my legs. My legs are wrapped in nappies.

My third sense is hunger. I haven't eaten for days. I'm starving. When I try to be sick, all I get is bile. I'm malnourished, dehydrated, hollowed out.

Pain, smell, hunger. The first three things that hit me every morning. But none of that matters.

Because my fourth thought kicks in.

Terror. I'm totally out of my mind with stress and horror.

Why? Because withdrawal is on me. I know it's going to get worse and worse as the day goes on.

What does withdrawal mean?

Physically, it means cramps, diarrhoea, vomiting. A whole body pain that consumes me. The body shuts down, only functioning to eject all the stuff in it until drugs hit the system again. I won't be able to do anything at all in a few hours.

Mentally, emotionally, it's crippling.

Meanwhile, inside my head, like a huge clock chiming deeply every second, I hear only two words:

'Heroin.'

And then,

'Crack.'

The terror overrides everything. It's more powerful than the crippling pain, or the stench, or the hunger.

The words and the terror of withdrawal take over my whole head.

They drive my day.

Just like they did yesterday, and just like they will tomorrow.

I've got to get heroin and I've got to get crack.

So my day begins.

The only way to delay total collapse is to feed the illness that's gripped me for years.

I've got to move. I have to get off the sofa in whichever drug den I ended up last night.

My legs are so painful that it takes me half an hour to swing them the seven or eight inches I need to put my feet on the stinking, needle-strewn, blood-soaked floor.

I ignore the used needles – dropped by people who've just passed out around me, letting them fall wherever they sit.

As I move my legs, the blood rushing back into the wounds on my legs increases the unbearable agony.

Each fraction of an inch takes a massive amount of willpower. I gag with each clench of muscle, feeling my stomach lurch up to my throat as the pain punches me.

I finally get my feet onto the carpet.

I'm wearing the same clothes I've been wearing for weeks. No change of boxers or socks or anything. I exist in whatever I've got on my back. My teeth are rotten and my fingernails are filthy.

Other smells now come at me in waves.

Drug dens stink of piss, of shit, of blood, of dirt, and of stale, sweaty clothes, and of bad breath and BO of the other addicts.

Beside the used needles and crack pipes on the floor, there are piles of clothes. Black T-shirts, black towels, black pants and socks. But black isn't their actual colour. They're completely stained with dried blood where people have used them to dab their puncture marks after they've injected.

The dried blood isn't just on the clothes. It's on the sofa, on the carpet – on any surface or fabric, soaked in. Blood from 10s of different people.

We used to share needles in these places. We'd get sharp boxes – sealed containers where you put used needles given to you by the pharmacy – for our needle-exchange programme. Most pharmacies in most towns provide this service for junkies.

You go in and sign up for the programme. They give you whatever needles you need – whether you're using 1 ml, 2 ml or the big 3 ml syringes. And they give you 30-40 of them.

But the deal is that you give them back in the sealed sharps box once you've used them and then you'll get a new batch.

I've cut open well over a thousand of these sealed sharps boxes in search of a needle – anything that wasn't too blunt to inject myself with. Putting my hand in a bucket full of bloodstained needles is risky enough, but pulling one out, rinsing it and using it to inject yourself is far, far beyond that.

I've most definitely used other people's syringes over 1000 times. How I never got HIV, I'll never know. I've been tested seven times, and waiting for the results each time was one of the most nerve-wracking experiences I've had.

Every time I look for another needle and stick it in my groin, I'm hoping that this hit out of the 50 I take a day won't kill me.

But the fix was literally the only thing that mattered.

Now I've got to get the nappy off my legs. Overnight, the inside of the nappy – the absorbent layer – has dried onto the open wound.

It's dried and it's stuck.

I have to drag my leg, barely able to lift my foot, trying to avoid putting any weight on my legs, to the bathroom.

I move carefully, trying to avoid the women sleeping on the floor. These women, a lot in their early 20s but who look more like 50, with rotten teeth, bodies shrunk to the bone, plastered in cheap make-up, are selling their souls against their will nine, ten times a night for a fix, because they are so gripped by this illness of addiction. When they get in, they collapse on the floor, their bodies, minds and spirits crushed, exhausted by the humiliating life they lead.

Everybody in the den is from all walks of life: rich, poor, black, white, Asian, from all over the country. They could be well-educated; they could have left school at 14. Just because you're a junkie, it doesn't mean you're automatically someone from a broken home or a council estate. Addiction doesn't discriminate.

I lower myself into the disgusting, bloodstained bath and run the tap. There's only cold water – there's hardly ever any hot water in a crack den. I start to peel the nappy off centimetre by centimetre.

As it slowly comes away, all I can smell is decaying flesh. My leg is rotten; the tissue is dead. It's as though I'm taking a dressing off a corpse that's been dead for a week.

I retch and retch, swallowing back the bile.

As I'm peeling it off, small chunks of skin are being pulled away, stuck to the inside of the nappy. The pieces of skin are half a centimetre thick by three centimetres long and as they lift, I can see my veins, tissue, cartilage, muscle and bone.

The cold water's running to try to wash the blood and dead tissue away.

After 10 minutes, I manage to remove the whole covering to expose the open wound on my leg.

My leg looks as if it's been hit by shrapnel or bitten by a shark. The flesh around the bone is completely black. Totally infected.

I wrap around another nappy and bind it with either Sellotape, masking tape, an elastic band or a shoelace. Whatever I can lay my hands on.

I put my filthy, stinking tracksuit bottoms back on. There's nothing to wash with, no toothpaste, no toothbrush and we use newspaper for toilet paper. Every penny that anyone has goes on drugs, except for the one absolute essential that was in every crack den I ever spent time in.

Sweet, milky tea. There are always teabags, milk and a 2 lb bag of sugar.

The only cooking stuff is a dirty old kettle and dirty old cups with the handles broken off and stained like a prison toilet with too much use. Disgusting, but the need for sweet tea overrides that too.

All the time, the voice in my head is shouting, screaming at me:

'Heroin. Crack. Heroin. Crack. Heroin. Crack. Heroin. Crack.'

I'm patched up enough to take the next step.

I've got to go outside and get to a phone box to call a taxi to take me somewhere to shoplift. The problem is I've knocked just about every cab company in the area. Most won't take me now unless I pay upfront.

I get one and when it arrives, I ask the driver to take me to Lakeside shopping centre in Essex. The taxi driver looks at me as soon as get in.

'What's that smell?'

'I've got a few infections in my legs.'

On the way, I get the cabbie to stop at an off-licence where I nick four or five cans of super-strength lager. I neck these as we drive to keep the pain and cravings away until I can get my fix. It takes the edge off the withdrawal.

But the shouting in my head is getting louder. I didn't think it could, but I'm almost blind with the noise.

Now the rest of the day is about luck and timing.

I could turn up 10 times to any of the department stores in Lakeside, and each time there might be a security guard on the doors. If there is one, I can't go and rob because I can't run like I used to be able to. My legs are too done in.

My whole focus is on getting some goods to fence so I've got cash to score some crack and heroin.

It's safer to try other shops where there are no security guards and where you can easily return things first. Some of them used to give vouchers for returned items so you could get what you wanted after.

I walk in. There's no CCTV or anything like that, so as long as I'm careful and quick, robbing is easy.

I take trousers, shirts, suits. All the higher-end items I can find. Within a minute.

I walk out with £2,500 worth of stuff. I phone my fence from a payphone and get him to meet me. He pays me 25% of the value of what I've nicked.

Next stop is to call the dealer. I get in the cab again and we head off to meet him.

By this time, I'm sweating badly, really badly. The cab driver's giving me the eye in the back as I curl up.

I meet the dealer and hand over most of the money. I get equal amounts of crack and heroin. It's late morning by now; I can see the next fix coming.

With the drugs in my pocket, sitting in the back of the cab, I can feel the bile rising again as my body starts to go into full withdrawal. I still haven't had any food – all that's left in my stomach is Kestrel Super.

I tell the cabbie to stop at a McDonald's and wait.

I've not eaten for four days and am severely malnourished. I should spend something on a burger, but I've spent every penny with the dealer on crack and heroin.

But I don't care about hunger. All I care about is the hit I'm about to take.

I run in, lock myself in the disabled toilet and cook up the crack and heroin. I inject, and my body rejoices in relief.

After the hit, I feel slightly normal again.

I get back in the taxi and go back to the drug den.

The stench of my leg, of the flat, of the rotting clothes and unwashed bodies is nothing now. I've got my drugs. Everything is going to be all right.

I strip back down to my pants, throwing the tracksuit bottoms and top on the floor with the other disgusting clothes. I do that so at least my clothes won't get even more bloodstained.

Then I sit there for an hour cooking up the crack and heroin and loading it into as many syringes as possible so I don't have to do it later when I'm off my nut.

I look around me now. At least the daylight hours are sorted.

Some of the guys I know. There's one new one. He's passed out still. Must have come in at some point the previous night.

Drug dens are dark, lonely places full of strangers all desperate to be out of the public eye so they can inject their drugs every day. Everyone's there to do the same thing, so there's no shame because we haven't got any shame left. We'll do anything to have the next fix, and we inject in front of each other all the time.

There's usually the hum of chat, everyone off their nuts, talking rubbish. No one's really listening.

If there's a television, it's black and white and ancient, but at least it's something else to look at.

It's on in the background as I reach for another syringe. It's a big one. I need a long needle to hit the only vein that isn't hardened to the point of cement – the one in my groin. Like I say, there's no shame among crackheads as I pull down my dirty, bloodstained boxers and hunt for the place to stab myself with the needle.

When you inject them together, the one that hits you first is the crack, and then the heroin kicks in when the rush from the crack calms down.

But while I'm awake and have crack cooked up, I just want the hit from the crack.

I reckon I've got about 30-40 hits to last me the day.

I'm obsessed with these fixes, though. By 7 o'clock, I've used it all. The voice in my head starts up again:

'Crack. Heroin. Crack. Heroin.'

There's panic in my mind that I haven't got anything until I go out grafting again.

I know that Lakeside is open until 10 p.m.

I go out again. Second round of grafting, fencing, dealing of the day.

When I finally run out of crack again – at about 3 a.m. – all the heroin that's been sitting dormant in my system kicks in and knocks me clean out.

And then the pain jolts me awake again, and my living nightmare starts all over.

I did this day in, day out for 15 years. In different drug dens all over the place. And I mean everywhere. There's a crack den in every single village, town and city centre. Just because you may live in a nice area doesn't mean for one second that there isn't a drug den around the corner. It's going on everywhere. Right now.

I was once a bright, bubbly 10-year-old full of life and joy. I only made it to 40 years old by sheer luck. Addiction, drugs and alcohol controlled and then destroyed my thinking and behaviour. I did not choose to live like this.

CHAPTER ONE

Eight-year-old Paul Hannaford knew exactly what he was going to do when he was older. He was going to play left back for West Ham, have a big house and be famous for his football.

He'd probably have a beautiful wife, kids and be a happy family man.

Almost certainly he'd live in Essex. That bit at least has come true.

Eight-year-old Paul Hannaford was a cute, cheeky, fun, energetic kid. He had curly blond hair, blue eyes and was popular with all the other kids. He loved his mum and adored his dad.

He loved his brothers – at that point there were three, Lee, Tony and Jamie, all younger – and had a large group of friends.

Eight-year-old Paul Hannaford was a normal kid.

I was born in a hospital in the East End of London in 1969, but before I was two we moved to Bruce Avenue in Hornchurch, Essex. It was just an average street with lots of families with kids and a lot of energy. There was a lot of love there, too.

From the moment I could walk, I was obsessed with playing in the street. Every weekend we'd be out there from morning to teatime.

On a Saturday morning, I'd wake up before 8 o'clock, get dressed and go and stand by the front room window, nose pressed against it looking at the street, thinking about the day ahead. My mum wouldn't let me out until 9 o'clock, but as soon as she opened the front door I was out like a greyhound.

I'd run down the road, knocking on my mates' doors, not waiting for them to open and come out, just moving on to the next one.

Slowly – too slowly for me sometimes – they'd all appear. There were about 15 or 20 of us, boys and girls.

By 9.30 a.m., everyone was out. We were on skateboards and bikes or playing football. By the end of the day, I was covered in cuts and bruises. Usually from trying to do a skateboard trick where I'd stack a few boards on top of each other and try to skate down the hill. It never worked, but it didn't stop me from trying.

I was first out and last in. My mum would try to get me to go in for my dinner, but I would just shout 'Five more minutes!' to her and carry on.

It took my dad, Ted, to come out – in his vest, cigarette hanging from his mouth, belt in hand – for me to take notice and finally go home.

Bruce Avenue had that old East End community spirit. Everyone's front door keys were hanging on a bit of string inside the letter box, so you just had to reach in and grab the key to unlock the door.

There was a huge amount of trust and all the parents looked out for all the kids.

Like I say, I was a normal kid who was well liked, who liked other people and was always up for having a laugh. And I got really enthusiastic about anything I tried. I even liked school.

My teachers thought of me as a bit of a lovable rogue. I had the blondest hair you've even seen, with curls, and a cheeky grin and blue eyes.

Dad was born in East London. He was a bit of a character – always had a story or a joke – and very bright: he could do *The Times* crossword in five minutes. Physically, he was athletic, stocky, powerfully built, with thick, curly black hair.

He'd been married before he met my mum and I had three half-brothers, Teddy, Barry and Kevin, as well as a half-sister, Beverly.

The important thing, though, about Dad was that to me he was God. I did everything I could to get his attention. It became, like a lot of things in my life, a bit of an obsession.

He worked as a supervisor for a groundworks company. So he was off inspecting what the builders had done all the time. Sometimes he went to work on a Saturday, and I leapt at the chance to go with him. Anything to have a bit of his undivided attention. He'd start up his Rover 3500, put Nat King Cole on the eight-track stereo and we'd head off to some factory or shop with 'When I Fall in Love' blasting out of the speakers.

On the way, he'd stop at the bookies and put a bet or two on. He won on the horses all the time. I can picture him in the betting shop listening to the commentary on the radio – they didn't have TVs in the shops then – rocking back and forward on the chair as if he was the jockey.

Dad was a gambler as well as a lot of other things. We lived a comfortable life because he and Mum got lucky on the football pools when I was about one. The pools is a nationwide betting syndicate based on predicting the football results. Back then, every week you filled out a paper form picking 10, 11 or 12 matches that you thought would end in a scoring draw (so 1-1 or 2-2). All the stake money was 'pooled' and the player with the most accurate predictions won the top prize, which was shared if there was more than one winner.

Dad won it by mistake. He'd put down the wrong result, but sent it off anyway and they won.

One of my best memories of him is me coming down for breakfast and he'd be sitting there in the kitchen in his white Y-fronts and white vest, slippers, roll-up in one hand, newspaper in the other studying the horses, cup of tea on the kitchen table and a pile of betting slips in front of him.

What that did was give him and Mum spare cash for parties and having friends over – there were always people coming round. Dad was always the centre of attention – the life and soul, very funny and full of energy.

If he didn't have friends at our house, he was in the pub – either The Cricketers or The Compasses in Hornchurch. My brothers and I weren't allowed inside, so he'd bring us a bag of crisps and a Coke every hour while he sat and drank with his mates.

For me, growing up was all about my dad. He was the reason I did everything. And I'd do anything to get his attention.

He had a shed at the bottom of the garden where he'd store all his tools. I'd go in just to touch some of them and move them around. He'd come back and give me a telling off, but that was fine by me.

Dad also loved his boiled bacon and pease pudding, and his shellfish – cockles, winkles, all of them. He used to send me round to buy cockles and winkles from a fish stall.

Cockles and winkles are a pain to prepare. They come in pints with their black shells on. What you have to do is get a pin, dig it into the soft part of the shell at the bottom and dig out the flesh.

Dad couldn't be bothered to do that, so he'd get me and my little brother to do it. We'd spend hours shelling them. We didn't care; we were doing it for the man we worshipped. We'd have done anything he asked.

When we'd finished, he'd put them in a bowl, add some vinegar and pepper, get some bread and make a winkle sandwich.

It was 1977, the year of the Silver Jubilee, and my dad set up a fancy-dress party for the whole street. There were parties like this happening all over the country, but this felt special as it was ours.

The downside was his great idea of dressing up me and my brother Lee as Robin Hood. We had to wear this green outfit with tights, and I was so angry with my dad because I thought I looked more like an Oompa Loompa than Robin Hood. But in the end, it didn't really matter because I did it for my dad. He was my God.

And being only eight, I forgot about it as soon as we started playing. We had the time of our lives. There was all the food that kids love to eat: ice cream, sweets, sausages, all of that. And none of the parents took any notice because they were having their own knees-up.

Dad loved football and he loved West Ham. Like I say, he was a proper man from the East End of London.

At that time, it was just the beginning of West Ham's golden age with players like Brooking, Devonshire, Bonds and Lampard coming into their prime.

So football became another way of getting my dad's attention.

In the same year as the Jubilee, I joined a football team called EMH (Essex Minors of Hornchurch) and, like everything I do, I got obsessed. I practised for hours in the garden or out on the street. If my dad came and joined in, I was made up.

I'm left-footed and played left back. I wasn't very fast, but I was solid, chunky, skillful and could read the game, so I was difficult to get past.

On Monday and Friday nights there was practice in Upminster, and then every Sunday we'd have a match. Dad came along when he could, which made my weekend. I'm not being boastful when I say I was good – we lost most of the times I couldn't play.

And at the same time, of course, I got interested in West Ham. It was in Dad's blood, so I automatically adopted them, too. I'd watch Match of the Day every Saturday night and hope that West Ham were on.

My favourite players were all those who became legends of the club: Trevor Brooking, Frank Lampard, Alan Devonshire, Phil Parkes and Billy Bonds.

I lived in my West Ham kit whenever I wasn't in school uniform. My dad had bought it for me, so it had even more value in my eyes. And I really wanted to play for them. It was my earliest ambition, and one that has the most regrets for me – perhaps because it was so closely linked to my dad and the life I had back then.

While my life was all about Dad and the street, my mum, Bonnie, was a big part of it, too. She was a good mum who looked after us and kept us in line.

She had a naughty stick – a bit of bamboo. I was always getting that rapped on my arse for being bad, but it wasn't vicious; it was just something that parents did in those times.

She cooked, cleaned, made sure we did the right thing. She gossiped with the neighbours and tried to call us in for tea when we played outside. But she knew that the only one who could really do that was my dad.

Mum and Dad met in the East End. Mum was a telephonist, working at a telephone exchange, and Dad had been a tank driver in the army, which was probably why he was so fit. They seemed really happy.

My other obsession when I was at primary school was swimming. Me and my mate Sean used to spend hours and hours in Hornchurch swimming baths at the weekend – only running home at lunchtime to have our dinner before running down the hill back to the pool. Our mums used to take it in turns to feed us. And then they'd torture us by making us wait an hour for our food to digest before letting us go back.

The thing about me at that age was that I was enthusiastic about everything. I even loved primary school. I wasn't the most able student, but I joined in with all the activities, put my hand up even if I didn't know the answer and just wanted to be around people.

One of my teachers, Molly, lived next door to us. She was a music teacher who was a very kind, but maybe very naive woman, very well spoken, with this BBC accent, which stuck out like a sore thumb in Hornchurch. She was religious, but also into her flower power and living green – even in the 1970s.

Looking back now, she was a bit like a hippy Dame Vera Lynn.

But when my dad was late for work or couldn't take us to school because he was away, or we were late because my brothers were being slow, instead of walking, which I loved doing, my mum would say, 'Right, Molly'll take you.' I wouldn't have it. If I got spotted turning up to school with a teacher – Molly in particular – my mates would ruin me. My street cred would go straight out of the window. But some days I didn't have a choice.

So we'd get into Molly's old beige Ford Cortina moaning and complaining to my mum, who just ignored us. Then the journey to school was so slow, if felt as though she drove at about 2 mph.

That made the torture of arriving in her car even worse. My mates would slaughter me, and I'd go home fuming at my mum for making me go with her.

Molly had apple and pear trees in her garden, and she used to make her own jam. She must have liked me a bit because she used to invite me in to help. Sometimes I'd go; I didn't mind it really. It was something else to do and none of my mates would find out, so it was harmless enough.

One day, I heard my mum and dad talking in the kitchen about our local pub, The Cricketers. The landlord and his wife had recently got divorced. At that time, the brewery who owned the pub didn't like divorced or single men to run pubs. The temptations of drink were too big.

Mum and Dad were always in there, so when they heard he was going, they started talking about whether to take it on.

They decided to go for it. They sent off the application – I don't know whether they had an interview – but about two weeks later, I got home from school and my mum said, 'Listen here, we've got some news. We're moving into The Cricketers.'

We rented out the house and moved into the pub.

I'd just turned 10.

It was a great childhood. Things started to go wrong a few years later, though. But could 10-year-old Paul Hannaford have predicted what would happen over the next 10 years of his life? Never. If anything, I was happier at that moment when we moved into the pub than I'd ever been.

CHAPTER TWO

I can't imagine how happy my mum and dad were when we moved into their local, but I know for me it was like moving into paradise.

From living in a three-bedroom house where I shared a room with my brother, we now had the run of this massive pub.

I got my own bedroom at the top of the pub – it was huge. There was a big window looking down onto the street.

We quickly settled into a routine. Mum and Dad were in their element.

Mum ran the bar while Dad would sit drinking and chatting with the regulars. He was like the pub host. Every now and again, he'd have to get up to change a barrel or a bottle of spirits, but he mainly entertained and told stories – looking as though he'd been a landlord all his life. He was a natural.

As far as I was concerned, The Cricketers had everything I could want: a pool table, fruit machines, Coke and crisps. And us kids were allowed the run of the place.

There wasn't all-day drinking back then. Pubs used to have to shut in the afternoon from 2.30 p.m. to 5 p.m. So after school I'd take all my mates back, and we'd be left to do what we wanted. Mum and Dad would be out shopping or having a rest.

We'd get a stack of beer mats, roll them up and stuff them down the pockets of the pool table so the balls didn't drop all the way down. Then we'd pay for one game and spend the afternoon playing pool, eating crisps and drinking Coke which I'd just take from behind the bar.

My brothers had their mates back, too, so it was like a big indoor playground for us all.

In the evenings, I very quickly got to know the regulars.

They were a mixture. Some were tradespeople like bricklayers, plumbers, painters and decorators. They were good old and young blokes having a few pints after a hard day's work.

And then there were two other distinct groups. They were very different in terms of the age and profile of the men, but with one thing in common: they dressed smart.

The first were the West Ham fans. They used to take me to games on a Saturday, which I loved. My mum warned them, though, that I wasn't allowed to get into any trouble. If I went with them, they'd have to look after me. They did.

The second group were the old-fashioned East End gangsters. Proper crooks and villains with reputations. These characters were old-style criminals, making money however they could. Most of the scams involved either fraud or money laundering.

They'd turn up in their posh suits and Rolls-Royces and play Kalooki – a card game that was a bit like rummy. It was really popular with East End families.

And the villains adopted me as a sort of errand boy for them. I'd get bottles of light ale to go with their lager (light 'n' lager was their preferred drink) from the bar, or run across the road to the newsagent for cigars, cigarettes or rolling tobacco like Golden Virginia or Old Holborn. They'd pay me tips for each errand. And I ended up saving a lot of money.

That was despite the fact that I hated cigarette and cigar smoke. Really hated it, but I'd just sit there with them on a Saturday waiting to get an errand to run. I had a box under my bed where I kept all the tips.

I was just a 10-year-old kid earning some good pocket money for running errands.

The atmosphere in the pub was all right most of the time. The locals, the football fans and the criminals all rubbed along OK, and Mum and Dad kept everyone happy.

There was trouble, though – and it used to get bad. The thing is that it wasn't much different from most other areas in London and Essex at the time.

But I think we were all having a great time. Mum and Dad were running a pub, and they loved being in pubs; Dad had his ready-made audience and Mum was providing for more than just her family. Living in a big house like that with so much space gave us kids room to run around and have friends over. And my parents had money from renting out the family home.

In 1980, West Ham were having a worse than average season. They were in the Second Division (the equivalent then of the Championship) and, despite having the team that everyone remembers best, struggled to finish in seventh place.

I like to think it was because they had such an amazing run in the FA Cup that they did so badly in the League. In the Cup, they beat West Brom (who finished third in the First Division that season), Orient, Swansea and Birmingham (all three also in the Second Division), Aston Villa (finished seventh in the First Division) and Everton (First Division).

West Ham made it through all those rounds and got to face Arsenal in the final at Wembley. Everyone in the pub and surrounding streets was excited.

One Saturday morning a couple of weeks before the final, an

envelope dropped on the doormat. Whatever was in it was quite stiff. It was addressed to Dad, 'the landlord of the Cricketers'.

I gave it to my dad who opened it up. Two tickets for the FA Cup Final from the brewery. I couldn't believe it. But my dad just stuffed them back in the envelope and put it in the safe.

I was devastated but, as it was my dad, I didn't say anything. Whatever he did was right.

Mum must have noticed something, though. That night at tea, she persuaded him to take me instead of selling them.

As a boy growing up in the 70s and 80s, there wasn't anything much more exciting than the Cup Final. Especially if you were as obsessed with football, and West Ham in particular, as I was. The fact that they made it to the final and I had a ticket to watch it was the icing on the cake.

I must have been unbearable to my mates for the next two weeks. Even at the most boring of times, I was a bundle of happy energy. Now I was stoked up with a Cup Final ticket and a day out with my dad.

When the day of the final arrived at last, I felt like it was Christmas morning. I put on my West Ham scarf and bobble hat even though it was late spring and going to be warm.

Mum made me a pile of cheese and ham sandwiches wrapped in tinfoil.

And then I got in my dad's Rover. He put on Nat King Cole and we went off on a massive adventure.

We got to Wembley, parked up and went into the ground. The seats were fantastic – just above the dugout so you could hear what everyone was saying and I felt, even at Wembley, so close to the pitch.

West Ham played in white – their away colours – and Brooking scored with a header after 13 minutes. I think it was the only goal he ever scored with his head. We went mad. The whole West Ham end singing 'I'm Forever Blowing Bubbles'. I'd never experienced anything like that joy.

The rest of the game was a complete blur apart from I remember Paul Allen – the youngest player to appear in a Cup Final at that point – being fouled by an Arsenal player, Willie Young, just as he was moving in on the Arsenal goal to score a second.

It was only two minutes until the full-time whistle, and we were convinced that he'd score and we would be in the clear.

Young only got a yellow card.

As soon as it happened, Dad insisted we leave the ground so we could escape before the traffic.

We raced back to the pub and had a massive celebration. The West Ham fans were out in force and the drink flowed well into the early hours. Me and my dad were centre of attention because we'd been there. I must have replayed Trevor Brooking's header 100 times.

Dad took more money that night than any other.

True or not, I do know that he took thousands that night because the following day, the Sunday, I helped him cash up.

I often used to do that on a Sunday. It was another time I could spend time with him. The pub would take thousands a week. And it was all cash – there were no credit cards or touch payments then.

With the money I'd saved from the gangsters, I went to the Army & Navy store really close to the pub. I bought myself the white away kit worn by West Ham when they won the Cup.

Later on, I'd take my mates to the Wimpy with the money.

'Do you want a magician for your birthday party?' my dad asked me about a month after the Cup Final. But I was already getting past that age. Besides, I'd had one a few years before and was bored.

'How about I take a few mates to the Wimpy?'

'OK. Get five of your friends and go and have a good time. I'll settle up with them later.'

Sweet.

Except I took the whole class to the Wimpy. Twenty-five kids. We ate everything. And I mean everything: chicken, fish, every kind of burger, milkshakes, cokes and lemonade. Then loads of puddings as well. We couldn't move.

The next day when I got back from school, my mum said, 'Better make yourself scarce. Dad's just gone over to settle the bill. He thinks he's paying for five kids.'

He gave me a proper hiding, but it was worth it.

If I were growing up now, doctors would probably have diagnosed me with ADHD (Attention Deficit Hyperactivity Disorder). But back then there wasn't any such thing – you were just a buzzing child who couldn't focus easily. I was a bundle of golden energy. And, I think, a nice kid.

Mum and Dad's attention was on the pub – in those days, parents were a lot less involved and not on their kids' cases as they are now.

Between me, my brothers and running the pub, there was more than enough stuff to keep them occupied. If they ever found out that I'd been naughty, Dad would discipline me if I was acting up or didn't do what he or Mum told me to do.

But when we moved to the pub, everything seemed pretty much set up right for them. They were both doing something they loved – my dad particularly – they had enough money and seemed to be living a good life.

And then, things started to slide. Dad's landlord act started to get out of hand, as he allowed lunchtime lock-ins for the gangsters. And I think that's where things started to go really wrong.

CHAPTER THREE

Now when I got home from school, all the villains would be sitting at the table in the dark because Dad had pulled the curtains across. They were playing their cards, but the atmosphere was heavier because most of them were drunk.

So were my mum and dad. They seemed to be getting drunk more and more. Particularly my dad.

At the end of each day, they'd both be pretty out of it.

Then they would have massive arguments. It used to upset me. I'm guessing a lot of it was related to or about alcohol.

I don't know how long it went on for – it didn't seem like a long time – but one day I got home from school and saw all the suitcases stacked up. Mum said, 'Come on, we're going.'

'What do you mean?'

'We've got to leave your dad.'

'I'm not going anywhere. I won't leave him. I love him. I can't leave my dad.'

We had a big argument. In the end she said, 'Suit yourself.'

And she walked out of the door with all my brothers and their stuff.

As a little 10-year-old boy, it totally confused me. I wanted to be with both Mum and Dad. It affected me deeply. Emotionally and mentally I was devastated, bewildered and shocked by the change. It made me doubt everything.

More than anything, it blew my happy, little, innocent world apart.

Dad and I were left alone in the pub just having the gangsters, football lads and other regulars for company.

Not long after she left, the brewery found out that Dad was on his own. And just like the previous landlord, they told him to go. So we had to go back to the old house.

He got his previous job back, but the drinking stayed. He was devastated that Mum had left. At that point I was left to do what I wanted, which wasn't very much. And shortly after that, Mum got social services involved. I was sent back to live with her.

Many months later, she got a new boyfriend. His name was Bob, a painter and decorator from Nottingham. We called him 'Nottingham Bob'. They rented quite a big house out in Poplar together. Moving into the house brought me and my brothers back together, and we were united by the fact that we hated Bob. None of us liked or respected him, so, being the eldest, I became a kind of father figure to them.

But I was totally confused by it all. Why wasn't I allowed to stay with my dad, the man who was my hero? Why did I have to live with this bloke called Bob who I hated? Why did I have to leave the school I loved and the mates I'd known since I was a toddler?

I had to leave EMH as well. And trips to Upton Park were finished. My love of football ended then.

Looking back, I can see the devastating effect of all of these things happening in such a short space of time. In less than a year, I'd gone from living a life that I loved to living a life that I hated.

My world had been blown to pieces. Not only had my God disappeared from my life, I'd lost everything that was familiar and that I loved too. No football, no West Ham, no dreams of playing football for a living, no school friends, no pool in the pub and no bedroom to myself.

Above all, I hated that I didn't see my dad regularly. In fact, after

I moved to Poplar, I didn't see my dad ever again. Can you imagine it? The man I worshipped just vanished from my life.

I was completely heartbroken. Even today it's hard to bear. To think you've only got your dad until you're 10 years old. That has a devastating effect on your life.

Although he was only in my life for that short space of time, I'll never forget him. His charisma, his love and his care for me.

Meanwhile, I think because everything in my life had changed for the worse, I had no idea what I was doing, what I was supposed to be doing or how I was supposed to live. My life had been turned upside down.

In my new school, Langdon Park, I started to rebel a bit. I couldn't concentrate, I had a massive resentment of my mum and her new boyfriend, and my football and my childhood felt like they'd been taken away from me.

I was increasingly angry and badly behaved. I got into fights and made myself unteachable. They kicked me out because I was unwilling to listen and do my lessons.

We moved again – I don't know whether it was because there wasn't a school nearby that would have me, but anyway, we went to Harold Hill in Essex. I went to my third school in as many years.

But again, I couldn't concentrate. My reading and writing were poor and the teachers, because they didn't know what to do, put me in special classes, which frustrated me. I was distracted and obsessed with what was happening to me and my family.

I'm not an idiot – far from it – but I didn't get school and I was going through a really bad patch at home.

All the while, I knew that I was looking for something. I didn't know what it was – but it was something to replace the perfect life I had lost when my mum and dad split.

I soon found it.

After school, I started to hang out with a group of boys. They were in the year above me – in Year 9 – and they were the in-crowd. Some of them lived on my street. We'd just get cigarettes and smoke, but then just after my 13th birthday I tried alcohol and cannabis. And I liked them.

I really liked them. I really liked them to the point that, in the space of a few months, I lost all interest in school, and in football. I may have stopped playing and going to matches, but it was still something I followed. Not any more.

I didn't bother turning up for school. I don't think my mum noticed or she was too busy with everything else going on.

Cannabis and getting money for it became the only thing I did.

I was expelled from the third school.

But when Mum and I started looking for a place for me to go, I found out that there was nowhere else that would take me except for something called a Pupil Referral Unit (PRU). These places were the last resort for the educational establishment. It was where they put children they'd basically given up on.

There were about 50 of us in this school – mainly boys but some girls, too – from all over the East End and Essex.

I realised pretty soon after getting there that the teachers may have meant well, but they had no control over us at all. So although I'm sure they did their best trying to get us back on track, to get us back into mainstream schooling, they didn't have the structure or authority to help us. After all, this was the place of last resort; they could hardly turn around and threaten us with expulsion, could they?

As a result, there were no boundaries at all.

The boys and girls in this unit were similar to me: all dysfunctional in some way. We should have been learning; instead, we were enjoying the lack of discipline in the PRU. Within weeks, me and some of my new mates were getting stoned and drunk during school hours.

After a while, there was a solid group of about 12 of us who hung out together. We separated slightly from the others.

The PRU, or the IT (Intermediate Treatment) Centre, was at Gallows Corner and on a bus route to Romford station, so after school we'd go and hang out there.

My life, in such a short space of time, was heading towards the darkness. I was walking unconsciously into a life that no one should lead.

And there were no guiding voices or attempts to bring me back on the straight and narrow. Mum was always having a go at me – but as soon as she did, I threw her leaving my dad back in her face. I blamed her for all of my actions.

When you're 14 and have no schoolwork, no after-school activities and no interest in your home life, there's a better than even chance that you'll go off the rails.

Our group started doing a bit of shoplifting and robbing stuff from the back of shops. Just annoying petty crime and we were a nuisance in the town.

Mainly, we'd go to a corner shop and rob as many cans of super-strength lager as we could: Special Brew, Tennent's Super, Kestrel – anything that was really powerful.

And then we'd drink till we were paralytic.

If one of us had money, we'd get the 84 bus from Romford to Forest Gate where there was a café called Lester's. The drug dealers used to hang out behind there, and we'd go and score our £5 weights of cannabis (it was cannabis resin back then – not as powerful as the skunk kids smoke now), and then take the drugs back to Romford and smoke it all.

So, by the age of 14, I was getting drunk and stoned every night. This was when my illness got a hold of me. Alcohol and drug addiction fuelled everything I did: the crimes I committed, the fights I was involved in and the desperate, sad, lonely life I was to have in my 20s and 30s as a result of my illness.

As if that wasn't enough, there was a brewery near the PRU. We discovered pretty quickly that around the back there was a loading bay where the delivery lorries parked up overnight.

Only a chain fence separated us from the crates of beer stored on the lorries. So after the brewery closed, we'd take some beer out of the lorries, chucking the crates over the fence, drink some of the beer and hide the rest in the bushes behind the PRU.

That meant the next day, at break time, we'd go drinking at the back of the school, returning to classes in the afternoon absolutely paralytic.

Like I said, what were they going to do?

The final straw came when, for some reason, the teachers decided to take us on a trip to Thorpe Park. It can't have been as a reward for good behaviour, that's for sure.

We properly played up the whole day but pushed even these teachers' patience by the end. The teachers told us that we had to go home, so we all walked back to the minibus.

But the staff were really dragging their feet. So while we sat in the van, waiting, they were taking ages.

We just got impatient, and one of us, a traveller guy called One-Eyed Bob, knew how to drive.

'Can't we just go?'

We all laughed, but he climbed into the driver's seat and started up the van.

We drove fast out of the car park and onto the motorway, with all the teachers left behind. We were bombing down the M3 towards London when up ahead we saw a lot of police. There were four or five cars waiting for us, and they managed to get us to stop.

The next day, we were kicked out of the PRU.

Expelled from the last chance saloon.

They didn't want to, but what choice did they have?

Now I was on the streets of Romford. No school or place of education would have me because there was nowhere else for me to go. I had run out of all options. My schooling was finished. At 14.

Nine of us from the PRU came together and formed a gang. It seemed inevitable, really – we had nowhere to go and nothing to do. I'm not saying that all PRUs created gangs, but if you start putting groups of dysfunctional boys together and don't impose any boundaries on them, then things aren't going to go well.

We called ourselves the East London Gang. I wanted us to be called the Essex Gang, but there were more of us from the East End than Essex, so it made more sense.

There's something reassuring about being with a group of other kids, belonging at a time in your life when you don't really understand what's going on. I had that problem made 100 times worse by having my idyllic life stolen from me.

No matter where we went, we just nicked stuff and caused agg. We were a dysfunctional group of black and white boys on the lookout for trouble.

My mum knew about it but, like everyone else, she couldn't control me. I'm not saying that if my dad had been around I wouldn't have tried the cannabis or the drinking. I don't know whether the trauma of them splitting up had an effect on me or not, but I think maybe my curiosity might've made me have a go.

I also don't know whether he'd have kept me on the straight and narrow as far as school was concerned. But at this point in my life, I had no idea where my life was going. Like most teenagers, I just lived for the moment. And we made the most of every single one.

CHAPTER FOUR

By the time I was kicked out of the PRU, Mum and Nottingham Bob had moved to Albert Road in Romford. She'd just had another son, Danny, so now there were five boys living in one house.

It can't have been easy for Mum, but I barely noticed. I was out with the gang all the time.

The core of the East London Gang was Danny, Big D, Little D, Nigel, Dave C, Alfie, Mark and me. We were out drinking, smoking and grafting on the streets of Romford using the KFC near Romford station as our base. The rest of the town was at our mercy.

The East London Gang was obsessed with booze and cannabis, and took every opportunity to get totally wasted. At the age of 14, I was living the life of an adult.

There was a particular gang member I was closer to than the others: Big D. Big D was a real unit. Even then he was 6 feet 6 and powerful with it.

Big D lived up the street from me. It was our daily ritual to meet at the end of the road and walk up to KFC where we saw Little D and Mark.

Getting stoned and drunk every day requires cash. So what do you do? You go out and rob as much as you can.

At first, we just shoplifted from local shops – small bits and pieces like alcohol, aftershave or cigarettes. Anything we could lay our hands on really.

But we needed to translate our haul into cash. Whether I remembered conversations at my dad's pub or whether I just picked up the idea easily, I don't know, but in a very short space of time I got to know most of the fences in the area. Some of them were shop owners, there was the odd car dealer, a publican and then there were the people who drank in the pubs.

Each of them liked something cheap, but we hadn't quite got to the stage of nicking to order.

So it started off just being easy stuff, but in a place like Romford you get known pretty quickly. Shop detectives in the department stores and shop owners in the smaller places saw us coming and were on their guard after only a few weeks.

And we were a group of 14-year-olds who should have been at school, so we stuck out like sore thumbs. The police were on to us quite quickly, too.

It was only a matter of time until I picked up my first prison stretch. I was still 14 and got nicked by some shop detectives.

Me and Big D had been working our way through the department stores. They were always the easiest to rob because they were usually pretty busy, and I reckon because they were so big no one really took much notice of the customers. The staff were bored and never paid much attention to what was going on.

We'd spotted some aftershave left unattended – someone was going to put it on display but had gone off for a break or something. I picked up the box and started running.

As I left, thinking that I'd got away with it, a plain-clothes shoplifting detective nabbed me. He grabbed me by the shoulder and, as I spun around, put me in a headlock and called for help.

I dropped the box and tried to wrestle him, but he was too strong.

Unfortunately, I was carrying my knife, as we all did in the gang.

I got three months for shoplifting and carrying a knife – in fact, it was for five separate offences, but they combined them all into one sentence.

The judge sent me to young offenders for three months for 'shoplifting and carrying a bladed implement'. I might have got off if I hadn't been carrying the knife.

As soon as I was given the sentence, I was sent downstairs to the holding cells until later that afternoon, when a minibus took me and a couple of other lads who'd been convicted of juvenile crime on a tour of other local courthouses, rounding up all the other kids who'd got young offender sentences.

We drove for about four hours with no heating in the van. Bars covered the windows. It was my first taste of not being able to do whatever I wanted. I was hungry and a bit frightened. After all, I was only 14 and had no idea what to expect.

We ended up at a place called Blantyre House in Kent.

The 10 of us arrived in the dark. All I could see were outlines of towers, fences and gates against the blinding brightness of searchlights. It felt scary. It was dark with lots of barbed wire and fences, and barking Alsatian dogs.

When we got off the bus, we were told to stand in line. A huge guy appeared who had the look of someone who'd been in the army. Straight back, powerful, immaculate creases in his clothes.

'Right, get your stuff.'

We were marched through large double doors and told to dump whatever we had with us. It was all labelled with our names for us to pick up when we were released.

The same sergeant major character lined us up in a row, like we were racing the 100 metres, and when he said 'Go' we had to race down a corridor to pick up what he called a 'bed pack'.

I got there – not first, but definitely not last either – and picked up my pack. It consisted of a blanket, pillow, clothes and a plastic cup.

The clothes were rank – they'd been worn hundreds of times by teenagers over the years. It was a uniform: work overalls, a shirt, boots and gaiters to cover the bottom of the overall legs and the top of the boots. And then there was your Sunday best – blue T-shirt, grey trousers and black shoes. You had to wear those for the governor's inspection every Sunday.

And then I was given my prison number. I won't ever forget that number.

Hannaford L85221.

It's lodged in my brain, and it'll go with me to the grave.

The prison guard marched us to our dormitory. There were three of them each with 30 beds lined up side by side. It was all very army-like.

I didn't sleep much that night. There were a lot of unhappy kids in the dorm.

At 6 a.m. there was a very loud shout and a bell rang. Another army sergeant major type strode into the dorm.

'Stand by your beds! Backs straight. Eyes front.'

He briefed us on our morning routine as we stood there like new recruits. Making our bed to exact specifications was one element of it. We had to strip off the blankets and sheets, fold them into a precise stack, flip them over and place them on the end of the mattress.

Our clothes from the night before (pants, socks, T-shirts) had to be folded, too. The guy actually had a ruler and measured the length of our socks once we'd finished our first practice.

After we'd folded and had everything measured, we were sent down to a room where three blokes with hair clippers waited. We queued to get our crew cuts. I couldn't believe it – my lovely blond hair. Half an hour later, it was all on the floor.

This was the start of the process to get us where they wanted us: lose our identity and make us all look the same. The system undermines your confidence and your sense of who you are. The idea is that it makes discipline much easier. But in fact, it's just a way of bullying and humiliating all the kids who are put there. That's not a way of rehabilitating anyone.

For the rest of the morning we were divided into two groups. One half did PE; the other did prison jobs. I got sent to the allotments in the prison grounds. There was other work as cleaners or in the kitchen or doing laundry.

My first job was to dig footings for polyhouses and then work inside them. It was June, so basically like working in a sauna.

When you're digging all morning you get quite muddy. An hour before we were called into the yard, the officer barked at us to clean our boots.

'You've got an hour. I want to be able to see my face in those boots.'

I thought to myself, 'An hour to clean a pair of boots ... it'll only take five minutes.'

They handed out boot polish and a brush.

There were about 50 of us in the yard, and I was chatting away to people but no one was really responding. They all had their eyes fixed on the boots, scraping off mud and polishing.

One other prisoner, a guy from Camden, who I'd got friendly with, finally came up to me. 'Listen, mate, you'd better clean your boots.'

I looked at him as though he was mad. 'But I've got an hour to clean them. It'll only take a couple of minutes.'

'You don't get it. If the bottom of your boot isn't as shiny as the top, and that guard can't see his face in it, they'll give you a hard time. And the gaiters have got to be cleaned as well.'

So I got to cleaning the boots, but I was a bit behind because of the chatting. After an hour, the guards shouted at us to put down our brushes and to line up with our boots in front of us. Three of them walked down the line inspecting the boots.

When it came to me, they stopped and looked at the boots. One of them leant into me. He was big, 6 feet 3 inches and 18 stone.

'Look at that. Get down on your hands and knees and look at that boot.'

As I went down, he stamped on my head, making me hit the concrete with my face. Then he put his foot on the back of my neck, pressing my face harder down into the floor. He maintained the pressure while telling me that I was a waste of space and a useless kid. A fully grown man doing that to a 14-year-old boy. Again, it was all about humiliation.

'You've got twenty minutes.'

When I got up, my head and face were grazed and I had bruises around my eyes.

I was a 14-year-old kid being beaten up and humiliated by a fully grown man.

I was left in the yard by myself cleaning the boots. Every day after that my boots were spotless because I was terrified of getting another beating.

The screws were really hard. I got a few digs from them. Not all of them were bad, but most were pretty unforgiving. They'd scream in your face and beat you up – usually for something we thought was really petty or minor.

One time, on a Sunday, I was standing in line to be inspected by the governor, so I had my Sunday best on. The guard told us every week to keep our hands out of our pockets, but I always forgot.

This big guard – a couple of us called him Redbeard because he had a huge beard and a very red face – was on duty. I was standing in the queue, and he reminded us to take our hands out of our pockets. I did that and then just forgot about it and put them back in.

Redbeard went mental at me. He dragged me out of the line and started slapping me hard around the back of the head. After about 10 slaps, I went down, and he started kicking me as I lay on the ground, curled up.

I kept my hands out of my pockets after that.

The guards were all about keeping absolute discipline – it didn't matter what tiny 'crime' you committed, or even if there was no crime at all. Their authority could never for one second be put into question.

Once I had a couple of run-ins with the guards, I started to work out the system. If you behaved yourself, did your job, kept your mouth shut and didn't step even a fraction out of line, you'd be OK.

Every Sunday there was a governor's visit. So all of us had to wear grey trousers, black boots, blue prison shirt and a jumper. I hated wool. I get really itchy if I wear it against my legs, so I managed to get an extra pair of pyjama bottoms to wear underneath my prison overalls and these grey trousers.

The governor would walk into the dorm, pick on one of us and give us a really hard inspection. Measuring everything; checking the shininess of the boots.

After a month of this routine, each prisoner was given a grading. The screws wrote a report on you every week: it had all the information about the way you behaved, how you did on the kit inspection and the other menial things you were supposed to do along with how well you worked.

At my first grading, I got moved from a category C to category B. This came with a few privileges: the dorm was smaller (only six of us) and it had a radio. Also, we got seconds at lunchtime.

All the other prisoners just laughed. 'How did you manage to wangle that?'

I was also moved up in my work to what they called 'Gardener 1'. This just meant that I was now allowed out of the compound to mow the screws' gardens, but it also meant that I was a trusted prisoner. I also got a couple of quid more a week.

My mum came to see me after a few weeks. She was pretty upset to see her little boy in prison. My hair had all been shaved off and I was sat in the visiting hall with a table between us.

I'm sure she was looking at me as though she couldn't believe it.

I said to her, 'When I get out, I'm going to behave myself.'

But it was more to make her a bit happier than anything else. I didn't have any intention of behaving myself.

By that point, though, I wasn't so scared. I'd worked out the system and wasn't getting any trouble from the other boys. Some of the older ones (16- and 17-year-olds) liked to push some of the younger kids around, but I was funny and chatty and they liked me. The ones they went after were the gobby ones who wanted to make a name for themselves.

The gardening job was a laugh. It was summer and I was out all morning in the sunshine sitting on top of one of those mowers that are like tractors. One time I lost control of it and mowed everything in one of the screw's flower beds, but it didn't seem to matter.

The three months went really quickly.

Looking back on the experience and all my other prison experiences, it's clear to me that there was never any attempt at rehabilitation. This was all about punishment and keeping me locked up. No one gave a toss whether I learnt anything in there at all.

The day of my release, I was let out with three other boys who were 16-17. We got a travel warrant to get a train home.

We went to the local supermarket and nicked a load of booze. Five minutes after leaving the prison, I'd committed a crime. Then 15 minutes later, I was getting drunk on the train with the other boys. I was 14 years old and within an hour of being released from prison, I had nicked booze and got paralytic.

Three months of this strict regime and all of that 'work' had disappeared within an hour. The attempt at rehabilitation by force and bullying just hadn't worked.

And all the time I should have been at school, doing my lessons, playing football with my mates, but already drugs and alcohol were the driving force of my life.

The next day I was out with Big D shoplifting. He was taking the piss out of my hair – because I had none.

I settled back into my old habits very quickly.

We started to get more methodical and smart in the way we went shoplifting. Instead of just robbing locally where we were already really well known, we got a map of the surrounding counties and started to target different towns and cities. Once we'd been somewhere enough times that we might get recognised, we'd cross it off the map and move on to somewhere else.

There was no CCTV back then, so if the shop assistants or store detectives didn't catch us or recognise us, we were OK.

We tried to look more grown-up and respectable too. I started to wear smart gear from Fila, Lacoste, Cerruti 1881, and Farah. It was all meant to make us look less suspicious so shop detectives wouldn't automatically start following us when we went in.

In those days, if I saw some druggy lowlife in smelly, dishevelled clothes, I'd think to myself, 'What a loser. How could you go about looking like that?' I had no idea that I would one day soon be in their battered, dirty shoes.

We were all under the driving age and none of us could afford a car anyway, so we'd get the train to the town and then work our way along the high street.

The way it worked was that, as soon as we got to a town, we'd split up into pairs. Then we'd target different parts of the high street.

If one of us got a good touch, we'd take it in turns to go in until we'd got all we could from the shop.

The main thing we looked for – particularly in department stores and bigger, busier shops – were bunches of keys. Shop assistants used to leave them out on the counter all the time.

Once we'd seen the keys, we looked for the long key. That was the safe key. If you could get those keys off the counter, you could unlock the door to the offices at the back of the store and, when you're there, open the safe.

Sometimes there would be float money in the safe – a couple of hundred quid – and then sometimes there'd be thousands, literally thousands of pounds. Remember, we were only 14 or 15 at the time.

But we only had a small window to get out the back, rob as much as possible and escape. If it was cash, that was easy. But the other thing we liked to get was cigarettes – they were so easy to get rid of to fences and we could get good money for them.

They were usually kept in metal cages out the back. They were in manufacturers' boxes of 5000 cigarettes – 25 sleeves of 200 fags. Benson & Hedges and JPS were the main ones. If we found them at the back of the shop, we'd open the back door and leave that way. Cigarettes were a great earner.

We were at this seven days a week. Always coming back on the train loaded with nicked goods: jewellery, aftershave, cigarettes or cash.

One time, early in the morning, we were in a town in Kent.

Big D spotted that a jeweller's shop had its large cabinet in the window open from the inside. There wasn't anyone minding what was going on.

Big D walked into the shop, and I started trying to direct him to what I saw from the outside were the most valuable pieces of jewellery. Rolex watches, large diamond rings and anything else that had a big price tag.

But he couldn't follow my pointing and so just scooped up everything he could and walked out again. We sauntered off down the high street looking very calm with tens of thousands of pounds' worth of goods.

That job paid for a lot of drugs and a load of cans of Tennent's Super.

It wasn't always that easy. Security guards, police and store detectives often chased us out of shops. But we were young and very smart, so they didn't stand a chance.

One Saturday, late afternoon at about 5 p.m. near Christmas, I was chased out of a department store by shop detectives. I had nicked a pile of women's coats (nine or ten, I reckon – probably about £1000 worth of stuff) and I couldn't really see where I was going I had so many of them.

As I walked out of the door, I heard, 'There he is – Hannaford. Get him!'

I think they were pleased because they'd spotted me in time, or so they thought. (They used to call me The Ghost because I just disappeared all the time.)

This time, I didn't even look behind because I knew who it was. I chucked all the coats on the floor and ran straight across the high street, a sharp left around the back of a load of shops and along the road.

I was running as fast as I could and thought I'd probably lost them by that stage, but I needed to hide for a bit just to let the dust settle.

I decided to go up to the snooker hall.

But I underestimated how fit some of the store detectives were. A lot of them were ex-army, so they were used to a bit of a hard run. There were about six of them.

I could hear them getting closer to me. I'm puffing by this stage. I got to the entrance of the snooker hall, then pressed and pressed the buzzer. They quickly let me in.

I pulled the door to and, as I did that, they came crashing into it. I ran up the stairs, into the bar area and out of the back exit and down the fire escape stairs.

By the time I'd got out the back, I thought I'd shaken them off.

But I was absolutely shattered. I walked down a caged stairway and out onto a road behind the shops. My aim was to go back to Romford station and get out of the area.

'There he is! Get the bastard!'

They were really close. I looked around and there was a multi-storey car park. It was busy – Saturday night around closing time for the shops, so there were lots of people leaving the town centre.

Instead of going up the stairs, which would have only led to the roof and nowhere to hide, I went through a door that was ajar on the ground floor.

As I pulled it shut behind me, the lights went on and there were five guys sitting in the room. They were road sweepers and litter collectors. It was their depot. They were all having a cup of tea at the end of their working day.

'Listen, do me a favour, hide me? I've just tried to pinch my girlfriend a coat for Christmas. Store detectives are chasing me.'

They looked at one another.

'All right, then.'

Just behind them was a little cloakroom.

'Hide in there.'

So I went into the cloakroom. No sooner had I got in there, I heard a lot of police sirens, dogs barking and coppers arriving. A load of commotion.

One of the guys went out to take a look. He came back in and said, 'There are about ten police cars, four dogs and the store detectives. They're searching every single car as it leaves the car park.'

The commotion was getting worse as the cars backed up and the drivers started blasting their horns.

Obviously, the police thought I'd jumped in a car and was trying to drive out.

After about 40 minutes, the guys said to me, 'We've got to go. Sorry, but we're done for the day. We want to go home. Can't stay here forever.'

I thought to myself, 'What am I going to do? I'll get nicked as soon as I walk through the door.'

I looked around and saw all the yellow and orange waterproofs and protective gear they wore hanging up on hooks around the room.

'Can I borrow some of that? I'll bring it back tomorrow.'

They looked at me a bit funny – I'd just told them I'd been trying to nick stuff, after all – but then they agreed.

So I put the gear on, pulled the hood up and grabbed a bag out of their bin, tied it up in a knot, put my head down and went out.

As I opened the door, my heart was in my mouth. I had no idea if I was going to make it through. I kept my head down, and all I could see were the boots of the police officers and the paws of their dogs.

I walked past them. No one said a word.

I got to the corner and a few of my mates, who were hanging about wondering what was going on, saw me.

'What the hell are you doing dressed like a bin man, Paul?'

And then they just started laughing while I told them the story.

I think a lot of luck but quite a lot of street sense got me through that. I was only in my mid-teens remember. The street was my school and I was good at some things.

Like making money by shoplifting usually – we made really good money.

And offloading the stuff was so easy. We quickly understood what different people wanted. The car dealers loved Barbour jackets. Clothes were popular with everyone. One sandwich shop owner still has a Jeff Banks suit I nicked for him 30 years ago.

Our department store searches focused on the big brands: Boss, Armani, Yves St Laurent, Pierre Cardin and all of those types of designers.

Once I'd fenced the gear, we'd jump on the 84 bus again – just like the days after the PRU – and head to Lester's.

After a few months of just smoking and drinking, though, we started to experiment a bit: LSD and magic mushrooms.

I loved mushrooms. For some reason they really got to me. I did a ton of research and even bought a book about them to make sure we picked the right ones. We went for Liberty Caps, which were the most common hallucinogenic ones, and managed to avoid those called Death Cap, which obviously wouldn't have been so good for you.

We spent a lot of autumn mornings heading off to fields to pick them. We'd collect bag after bag, dry them out and then take them.

Being me, I had to do the most out of all of us. We started off taking 50 or so. Most of my gang stopped there. But I just kept going, upping the numbers and getting more and more off my head.

I ended up in hospital twice after two bad trips. But still I kept taking more. That autumn of 1985, I was 16 and off my nut every day.

One night, I was at a party at my mate Smiffy's house. It was just around the corner – I mean, about 100 metres away from my mum's.

I decided to go for it and took about 500 mushrooms. By 11 o'clock, I was completely out of control.

Someone pushed me through the door of the party and pointed me in the direction of my mum's.

I'd done that walk so many times and it was really, really easy. You have to go along a road called Moss Lane, and my mum's house was on one of the streets off that.

The thing is that all the streets look pretty much the same – especially in the dark.

I set off, but then just got stuck. I don't mean scratching-my-head stuck, I mean stuck like I was on a treadmill – my legs were moving, but I wasn't going anywhere.

It felt like I'd been walking for about an hour when I finally decided that I'd died.

I thought I'd OD'd somehow on the mushrooms and my heart had given up. Now that I was dead, I was going to be stuck on this road forever.

I started screaming. I screamed and screamed and I screamed 'Help me!' just as loud as I could. I was in a blind, terrified panic.

One of my little brothers heard it at my mum's and got a couple of mates. Smiffy came out of his own party.

They thought I was in a fight. When they got to me, though, they just saw me standing, screaming:

'What's wrong? What's going on?'

'I'm trying to get to Mum's house! Can't do it! Stuck!'

They took hold of me and tried to get me to walk forwards. But I couldn't. Then someone had a brainwave. They turned me around and helped me to walk home backwards.

By the time I got there, I was still convinced I was dying. I got Mum to call an ambulance.

The police turned up, which meant that the rest of the gang ran off quickly.

I was tripping off my head when they arrived, and the sight of the uniforms nearly tipped me over the edge.

The police: 'What's going on?'

I looked at them blankly – Smiffy said my face was just total confusion. He was trying not to piss himself laughing in front of the police.

When I got to hospital, I sat there for hours. The nurses kept asking me my name and date of birth – just to keep my mind focused on something other than my hallucinations.

Next day?

I took acid.

Looking back at it, though, through the clear vision of being sober, the addiction, the illness that controlled so much of my adult life, had already taken control.

After young offenders' prison and the mushrooms, I'd like to think I'd had enough of a shock to take another look at my life. But I didn't. Me and the gang carried on – it was like there was nothing that could stop us.

Prison wasn't frightening any more, and it seemed that our bodies could cope with whatever we took. And my illness was telling me all the time to take more.

As far as the gang was concerned, we were invincible. There were constant fights with other gangs when they came into our area, but we rarely lost.

Drugs, crime and violence came easy to us and seemed not to have consequences. And there were no interventions from any parents; the police were after us, but we were usually just annoying to them – they had bigger fish to fry.

The point is at 14 we had no controls – either from outside or inside. We felt that we could do anything at all.

CHAPTER FIVE

And then just before I turned 15, I got kidnapped.

It was in the middle of my LSD and mushrooms binge, so I wasn't paying much attention to what was going on. I was only focused on the next trip.

A friend of the gang overheard a conversation that one of the boys he went to school with was always bragging about how his dad kept a load of money in a Portakabin in a yard by the side of a house.

We got the address of the house in a town nearby.

Three of us went round there one weekday morning when we thought everyone would be out at work. I waited on the street corner while the other two went in and got the briefcase.

As soon as the other two got out, we legged it to one of my old schools and headed for the playing fields. I remembered there was a huge bush where we could bust open the locked briefcase without being seen. It must have been during the school holidays. When I pulled the lid of the case up, we saw stacks of cash – a few thousand pounds in total – and a whole load of documents.

We couldn't believe our luck. Thousands of pounds for a 15-year-old in the 1980s was a hell of a lot of money.

We took the cash, divided it up between us and dumped the briefcase down a drain in the playground. Then it was off to the off-licence to get some cans, drop some acid and smoke some cannabis.

There wasn't going to have to be any shoplifting for a while, we thought, because we were loaded.

When you're not even 15 and you score as big as that, you never think about the consequences. I went out with my mates and treated everyone left, right and centre. Flashing the cash like I was a millionaire – which I thought I was. The whole gang, to be fair, were doing the same. Living it big. It all seemed too good to be true.

It was.

About three days after we'd broken into the yard to steal the briefcase, I was in the snooker hall, ripping off the fruit machines with Little D, when three big blokes appeared at the top of the stairs.

They came up to me and said, 'Are you Paul?'

Before I could say yes or no, they got hold of me. Dragged me off the machine. They were big fellas, casually dressed, so I immediately thought it must be the police, CID, coming to arrest me. But I didn't know what it could be for – I'd put the briefcase theft out of my mind.

These blokes took us to the bottom of the stairs but instead of throwing us in the back of a police car, there was a plain white van parked on the street.

One of the guys smashed me in the face, nearly knocking me out, and chucked me in the back of the van. Little D followed with a bloody nose.

The van pulled off. And my mind started to race.

'Shit, this ain't the police. Who are these men?'

I didn't have much time to think because after two or three minutes the van stopped, the doors opened and I could see that we'd parked in a car park outside a youth centre.

Opposite was the house we'd robbed.

One of the guys left the van, went into the house and then came back.

There were about four or five blokes hanging around, so there was no way I could run. They were big, with the look of people you didn't want to mess with. I remembered the regulars at The Cricketers and thought that they probably knew them somehow.

A couple of them took Little D into the house and kept me in the van. My hands and feet were bound with wire. It cut into my wrists and ankles – it hurt like hell.

One of them leant over me and looked me hard in the eyes.

'Listen to me very carefully. Don't bullshit me. We know you robbed the house. We ain't bothered about the cash. Tell us where the briefcase is, we'll let you go.'

I always learnt growing up in gang life that you kept your mouth shut. No matter what. So that's what I did. Besides, we'd robbed the place and dumped the briefcase three days ago. What was the possibility that it was still in the drain in the school playground? No chance at all.

The panic started to rise in me.

I didn't admit to the burglary. Kept my mouth shut, as the gang was more important to me than anything. And I had this one thought that if I pleaded ignorance, somehow or other they'd let me go.

The guy left, and I exhaled for the first time in 20 minutes.

And then another huge guy got in, shut the door behind him, raised his fist and beat the living shit out of me. Smashed me to pieces. I think he must have used a knuckleduster because each punch hurt like I was being hit with a hammer.

My face was mashed – eye socket damaged, nose ripped to shit – and ribs bruised within an inch of breaking. It must have gone on for 10 minutes.

He gave me the hardest beating of my life.

And then, as quickly as it started, it stopped. He jumped out of the van, slammed the doors and left me to my wounds.

The hours started to tick by. No one came into the van. All I could hear was some of the men walking backwards and forwards from the house to where the van was parked. They were talking and laughing, but I couldn't hear what about.

My body was screaming with pain. Every time I took a breath, my ribs flared up and made me gasp. When I put my hands up to my face, all I could feel was torn flesh and blood. I felt like puking every time I breathed.

My clothes were bloodsoaked and the floor around me was a mess. I'd wet myself a few times because they wouldn't let me use the toilet.

It was getting dark when two of them got into the front seats of the van and started it up.

The effect of the beating was deep – I didn't know what was going to happen and I was terrified.

For a brief moment, I hoped they were going to take me to hospital and dump me, but as soon as we pulled out of the car park we turned left. I knew the hospital was off to the right.

Looking back, I realise that I was just a kid of 14 who had no idea how adults behave, what they do and what these kinds of adults do if they've got beef with you.

With the faintest hope of being taken to hospital now squashed, I started to have a proper panic attack. I was terrified.

About 20 minutes later we were still driving. Finally, after 40 minutes, the van stopped.

The guys jumped out of the front seats, opened the doors and hauled me out. We were by a lake in a quarry.

One of them had a weight in his hands – like a weightlifting piece of equipment – the other had a rope.

'We're going to drown you. Tie this weight around your ankles and drown you.'

Faced with death, I said to the guy, 'Please, don't kill me. I'll tell you where the briefcase is but don't kill me.'

Whether they were bullshitting and this was their last attempt to get me to talk or whether they were going to do it, I don't know. But I honestly thought I was going to die.

I told them where it was. Or where it was three days ago.

That night in the back of the van, I prayed more than I've ever prayed in my life. The journey back to the school seemed to take forever. My body was throbbing, broken. I was panicking and my life, I thought, depended on the briefcase being where we'd left it.

I had no way of knowing before we got there whether it was. In my mind, I was imagining it not being there and what would happen next. I was terrified. All I could do was see the negative.

We arrived. Parked up. They pulled me out of the van so hard that I fell flat on my face. My legs and arms were still tied with wire. They yanked me to my feet and said, 'Show us.'

I limped to the drain and nodded.

One of them bent down and picked up the cover. I gulped and felt my stomach coming up.

He looked up at me. Holding my gaze, he reached down into the drain, pulling one sleeve up with his other arm to keep it from getting dirty.

And pulled up the briefcase.

It was still there. The documents were there, too.

I turned around and threw up. All the tension of the past 14 hours gone. I knew they'd let me go now.

We left the school, drove for 10 minutes and then they stopped. They undid the wire around my feet and hands and threw me out of the back of the van. And drove off.

I walked back to my mum's. She said, 'What's happened?'

'I've been in a gang fight.'

She took me to hospital, where I stayed for a few days because my face was in a really bad way.

When I got out, I was back with the gang. Big D and the rest of them saw the state of my smashed face. I told them I'd been kidnapped, and they were quite angry.

'Are you OK?'

'Yeah, and I didn't grass anyone.'

They had let the others go because they had some loose connections with the family.

When I told the gang what had happened, and admitted that I'd told them where the briefcase was, they said, 'We don't care, just as long as you didn't grass on any of us.'

Because of that, I was elevated a bit and got more respect in the gang.

If anything, then, surviving the experience made me feel better about myself. It had earnt me more status in the only thing I cared about – the gang – and I felt that I'd passed some sort of test.

It was another step towards being a gang leader. You've got to understand that a gang leader isn't necessarily the toughest, but the most trusted.

I was really frightened at the time, I can't deny that, but as a kid, if you get through something like that, you forget how it felt at the time. Instead of thinking, 'This life is dangerous,' I felt like I was a proper villain. Someone who mixed with gangsters; someone who took them on and survived.

And it really didn't look that difficult. We were good at shoplifting and our systems were getting better. We had a laugh when we weren't grafting and didn't get much agg from anyone else.

CHAPTER SIX

After the kidnap and escape, Big D and I got really tight. We were an inseparable unit – heading off shoplifting together, doing our drugs and drinking the proceeds of our crime.

His family were well known and had a reputation. He could really fight.

We were always out on the rob, so it wasn't such a surprise when I got nicked again. This time for handling stolen goods (the ones we'd robbed of course), possession of a controlled substance (ecstasy now) and carrying a bladed weapon. Like we always did.

Carrying the weapon was just stupid. Like I said, it only really came in handy if things got really rough and we had to up the threat of the gang to the people we were fighting.

The rest of the time – the majority – they just caused us more problems. Without the knife, I would have got off with a caution a lot of the time I was arrested. The police weren't that bothered about a bunch of kids who went shoplifting.

The second time I ended up in young offenders, I was taken to Hollesley Bay in Suffolk. I got four months there.

It was the same routine: make a dash for your bedding and cup, get your head shaved, shine your boots and get ordered about by ex-military screws.

I knew the drill a lot better, but the food was still terrible.

The daily menu didn't change: porridge, and bread and jam for breakfast. Lunch was half a chicken leg, under-boiled potatoes and cabbage. No pudding. For dinner there was usually a pasty or chips. And pudding. I really looked forward to teatime. Always loved my sweet stuff.

When I got out, me and Big D carried on knocking about together. Just like after the first sentence. Nothing changed – we were still out grafting, going to Lester's for cannabis or ecstasy or hunting magic mushrooms, getting off our nuts and starting again the next day.

I was 16 by this point, still living with my mum, Nottingham Bob and my brothers. Things were a bit calmer at home now. I don't know whether Mum and Bob had given up on me so weren't on my case any more, or whether we'd just learnt to tolerate each other better.

It didn't matter; we rubbed along in the house. The police were always knocking on the door, but that didn't seem to bother Mum much either. I wasn't there much during the day or the night. I'd crash back in late at night, be up after Bob and Mum had gone to work and my brothers had gone to school.

And then something life-changing happened.

I met a girl called Joanne. She had long blonde hair, big blue eyes and was just a year younger than me. From the start, we got on and seemed to understand each other.

She was 15. We started dating. My first proper girlfriend.

Seeing her after school and trying to keep up with the gang put a bit of a strain on both ends. If I didn't hang out with the gang, they'd give me a load of abuse and I would be a bit worried that my standing would go down; but if I spent a night out with the gang, then Joanne would get the hump.

She was pretty good, though, and tolerated my binges.

As I approached my 18th birthday, me and Joanne had been together for a couple of years. The temporary truce that Mum,

Nottingham Bob and I had called was fraying and we started rowing massively again.

I think it was probably all about the resurfacing of resentment about my dad. I was really pissed off with Mum – the way I thought she'd treated Dad and thought that she was the reason he wasn't in my life any more. Meanwhile, she and Bob were getting pissed off with the fact that the police were round every week looking for me, after me for some violence or shoplifting, something antisocial anyway.

Or it could just have been that the moment I became an adult was coming up and the tension about what would happen to me was getting to everyone.

I was really excited about being 18. It meant I could drink in pubs and buy alcohol legally and that I was finally a man. I couldn't wait.

Things got really bad. One day, I was round at Joanne's and talking to her mum, Kay, who I got on really well with. I was telling her about the latest row with Bob – something really petty or stupid as far as I was concerned – and she just said, 'We've got a spare room. Move in here.'

Joanne was 17 and I was 18, so that part made sense.

I leapt at the chance and moved in the next day.

Kay liked me back then. She thought I was a bit of a laugh, a bit of a rogue, which appealed to her naughty, rebellious side. I'm not sure after a few years she felt the same way, but at that moment it was a lifeline.

Sometimes your relationships with your parents seem totally beyond help. I didn't think at that point I could carry on living with my mum after what I thought was the betrayal with my dad.

So I moved in with Kay, Joanne and their dog, Roxy – a half-Alsatian rescue dog who was a big old lump.

Like a lot of stuff in my life, things were OK for a few months, and then I got involved in something that should have been a slight warning for Joanne.

I nicked a car. Or if I'm really accurate, one of the gang – or, truth be told, someone who tinkered around on the outskirts of the gang – nicked a car. He was called Bill.

He came round to Kay's one day when I was still 17 and said, 'I've got a car. Come on.'

'Nice one. Where to?'

'I've got a buyer already. Just need to drive it there to deliver it to him.'

'OK. Sounds all right.'

'Thing is, it's quite a long way.'

'Oh yeah? How far?'

'Spain.'

I pissed myself laughing.

Bill had nicked – to order – what was quite a flash car in those days, a Ford Granada Scorpio. It was the kind of car senior corporate executives drove or were driven around in.

The next day we got our paper passports – these were short-term passports that you could get from the post office. It was a single sheet of cardboard folded in three, about the same size as the regular passport, but was only valid for a year and you only needed proof of ID to get one. Most European countries accepted it and it was piss easy to get.

We left the day after that.

I didn't bother telling Joanne – I don't know why. We just packed an overnight bag, filled the car with petrol and headed for Dover. Bill drove as I hadn't passed my test.

We drove down through France stopping overnight in a small

town and getting wasted before carrying on through Spain down to the south coast and Marbella.

The thing about the Granada Scorpio, it was a really powerful but smooth ride. It had a 3.0 litre injection engine, leather seats, automatic gearbox and you felt like you were gliding when it was doing 100 on the French and Spanish motorways.

Of course, we'd got some cannabis with us and we smoked all the way down, music cranked up, having a laugh.

At some point as we were approaching the border with Spain, I dropped the lump of blow on the floor. I looked and looked as the customs gates got closer and closer, but I just couldn't find it.

It was getting dark and I was getting really paranoid about the drugs. We pulled over a few miles from the border and searched the car but it seemed to have just disappeared.

When you are really close to the border, you drive up a long hill and as you get to the top and look ahead, out of the darkness, there are all these bright lights illuminating the control gates and the approach to the checkpoints. It's like something out of a sci-fi film – hundreds of lights beaming at us.

As we got to the top of the hill and the lights shone brightly at us, we both panicked. There was no way we were going to make it through without the sniffer dogs or the customs officers finding the blow. We were in trouble, and that wasn't even counting the fact that we were driving a stolen car.

My heart was going mad, beating so fast that I thought it might explode. Bill was looking nervously all around to see how many cars were going to be driving up at the same time.

Then Bill gunned the engine and went through the exit gate, one without the barrier, and caused a massive alarm. All the guards started running towards us, guns held high, some of them with dogs.

I looked at Bill.

'We're blown.'

The first of the guards got to the car and motioned for us to get out.

We did.

'Passports.'

We handed over the flimsy bits of paper we'd got the day before. At this point, we were surrounded by guards and dogs. I was shitting myself about the cannabis and Bill, as he told me later, could see that one of the number plate fixings was broken.

They only needed to be a bit curious about that and they could look up the car or ring the police in the UK.

So he was shitting himself, too.

The guard looked at the passports as if they were used toilet paper, then looked at our pictures, and perhaps we were lucky it wasn't daylight and our red-eyed stoned faces weren't so obvious.

He looked once. Then he looked again.

Nods.

'Go.'

We grabbed the passports, jumped in the car and drove off.

I was 17, Bill was 18 – and they let us through in this big, flash Granada Scorpio.

As soon as the border lights disappeared in the rear-view mirror, Bill pulled the car over and we totally lost it. Pissing ourselves laughing, almost crying with relief. We couldn't believe we'd got away with it.

Then Bill gunned the engine and we hammered it through the night to Torremolinos.

We found a little Spanish hotel. In those days, you had to hand your passport over when you checked in. So we left our only documents there and were going to use what little money we had left to party in Torremolinos for a couple of nights.

It was all going to be fine, though, because on the third day we'd drive to Marbella, hand the cash over and pocket £3000. So if we had absolutely nothing left when we headed to do the deal, it didn't matter.

We ran riot in Torremolinos. Spent every last penny we had. Drove the car all over the place pissed up. But Bill was careful and the car, although a bit mucky inside, was immaculate outside.

On the third day we got up, hungover but happy, and headed out to get the car.

It wouldn't start.

Bill turned it over and over, but all we got was a dead roll. After 10 minutes, we opened the bonnet. The engine was black and smoke was starting to rise.

The big ends had gone. We'd driven the car loads without thinking to put any oil in at all, so the engine had ceased up.

The car was worth about 10p now.

We called the guy and told him what had happened. He sent someone over to check it out.

When he arrived, he took one look under the bonnet, shook his head and said, 'No chance.'

But, like the car, our trip was knackered, too. The hotel had our passports, we'd got no money to pay the hotel bill and they'd got all our laundry.

We were in a pair of shorts and a T-shirt, had no money and stuck in the south of Spain with no way of getting home.

The only thing we could do was walk to the British Consulate in Malaga, which was about two and a half hours away in the boiling hot sun.

We sweated our nuts off getting there, and then had to wait ages for them to see us.

'We've lost our passports.' And then invented some bullshit about getting ripped off in a bar and losing everything.

They gave us temporary passports but we still didn't have any money, so they allowed us to call Bill's mum who had to pay for our airfares.

We got on a flight the next day having slept rough in Malaga.

When we finally arrived at Heathrow, we got pulled aside as we were going through customs and taken into an office with a two-way mirror.

Some bloke in a cap and police-style uniform questioned us separately.

'What happened?'

'We just went out for a holiday.'

'How did you get there?'

'Some friends gave us a lift.'

Back then, there wasn't much in the way of checking these stories, so they let us go.

We'd got away with it. Didn't have the cash, but we'd had a laugh.

Joanne was less happy. When I called her from the airport, she was absolutely fuming.

It sadly set a pattern that would go on until my 30s.

Shortly after I got back, I turned 18. I was finally a man. I could now legally do all the stuff that I had already being doing. Mainly that meant, for me, drinking in pubs and buying lager from off-licences – when I wasn't nicking it.

Turning 18 also meant that I was an adult as far as the prison and justice systems were concerned.

CHAPTER SEVEN

18.

I'd dreamt of being 18 ever since I had my first can of lager, ever since I'd taken my first hit from a joint and ever since I'd had my first stand-up row with my mum and Nottingham Bob.

Being 18 meant freedom. It meant doing what I wanted. It meant independence. It meant living my life.

The night of my 18th birthday, I went to one of the local bars in Romford owned by a guy called Fred. In Fred's place, a lot of colourful characters did their drinking and some dodgy deals. He was a proper old-school East Ender. He made a big impression on me at 18 – it was as though he lived the life I wanted. He reminded me of some of the people in my dad's pub years ago.

Fred had a Rolls Royce but didn't use it much as he liked a drink.

He'd stand at the end of the bar. Immaculate every day in his suit; slim, gold-rimmed glasses; hair gelled back.

Fred was friendly with all the local well-known, old-time villains. So the pub had a sort of celebrity villain atmosphere. As well as some of the more famous or notorious criminals, there were local builders, run-of-the-mill guys who liked a bit of knock-off gear or liked to be around that slightly dodgy crowd, and street fighters and unlicensed boxers would come in, too.

What I grew to love about the place was that no matter when you went in, there would always be someone you knew. It was also a great place to fence the stuff we'd nicked.

Fred loved it when we got booze or cigarettes because he paid a quarter of the retail value and made pub markups on all the gear. For a while, he thought we were the best thing because we'd just bring him loads and loads of cartons of fags and bottles of spirits.

And suits. He loved a suit, and after a while he would ask me to get a specific one – Armani was his favourite. Boss and Yves St Laurent were the main ones back then, but any suit from a high-end store in the West End was also welcome.

I was there every night with some or none of the gang; it didn't matter to me because the regulars started to take me under their wing. There were always new scams and deals to get in on. One of them was very lucrative for quite a long time and raised my standing in the group and the pub.

I'd already started to wear the suits, I had immaculate teeth and still had good blond hair. I'd also started to bulk up a lot, so by the time I was 18 I was 18 stone. Thick and heavy set. Not unfit, but definitely on the heavy side.

Even before I'd bulked up, my nickname was Chubbsy. Sean Kelly gave me the nickname when I was about 13.

Anyway, one night in Fred's bar, one of the local characters approached me.

'All right, Chubbsy?'

'All right.'

'Interested in doing something new, Chubbsy?'

'Yeah. What is it?'

'Come with me.'

He sat down opposite me with his pint of lager top and said, 'The thing is, my mate has a girlfriend who's a postie, and one of her mates has put her on to a potentially nice earner. We just need someone to front it.'

'Go on. What is it?'

'Credit cards.'

'How does that work, then?'

He told me how credit card companies sent out replacement or renewal cards a few weeks before the old cards expired. The thing is that the card owner didn't know when it was being sent.

So when the postie felt a card in the envelope, he or she could just slip the envelope into a pocket and not deliver it. This was before the time of tracking or even chip and PIN. They used to just send credit cards through the post without any kind of attempt to disguise what it was. Before the internet, too, so there wasn't any online checking. If the card didn't turn up, the customer would just ring the credit card company to say they hadn't received it.

What that meant was this guy's girlfriend could just mislay a credit card and we'd have a window of about two weeks to max it out before the credit card company could do anything about it.

The credit card holder didn't suffer because they never received it. And the shops didn't suffer because the credit card company was obliged to pay them for the goods bought on the card.

Win, win, win. And a big win for me, this friend and his girlfriend.

I couldn't believe my luck, but I thought this through – like the shoplifting, there was quite a lot of planning that went into my crimes. My idea was that I'd buy upmarket goods with the cards – stuff that I knew I could fence easily enough and in shops where people were less suspicious.

To go into those shops, flash these credit cards and not stick out like a sore thumb in my Fila tracksuits and trainers, I needed to look and act the part. I needed to look like I had money. I needed to look like I belonged. The idea of playing the part really appealed to me.

And to make it even more convincing, I thought I'd need to turn up in a car. At the time, I don't know if I knew why, but now I think I was getting into character a bit more. Up until that point, I'd been happy using the bus or the train – public transport worked fine usually.

But now, to make the change, to make myself believe that I had money so I'd be more convincing when it came to using the cards, I decided that I had to be driven everywhere.

I had a mate called Jim. His nickname was Jewish Jim, which sounds a bit unsubtle, but he was happy with it. Jim was a huge guy. He loved his food and loved a bet – my picture of him is always of a guy with a pie in one hand and a betting slip in the other.

Jim was a bit older than me – about 22 at the time – and used to hover around the edges of the gang. There were a few of those kinds of people – they liked to hang out with us but weren't fully signed up or committed. Often they disappeared when things got a bit heavy either with the police or some other group of lads.

But Jim also had a car and he loved driving. So I gave him a job and paid him by the day.

When there was a card or two to use, he'd pick me up around 10 a.m. from Kay's. Kay was a dinner lady so she'd be off at work and Joanne worked for Brink's security company.

When I got up, I'd carefully put on a proper suit – I had a wardrobe full of Armani and Hugo Boss – and get myself properly done up. I looked immaculate: shining teeth, suit, tie, shiny shoes, pinky diamond ring, carefully shaven and blond hair Brylcreemed back.

That, together with my bulked-up frame, meant I also looked imposing, which is important when you're trying to get away with fraud. You've got to carry off the part, and people are less likely to be suspicious of someone who's big and confidently dressed than someone who looks timid.

Like in the old shoplifting days with Big D, I had a map of the local areas and ticked off the places where I'd already used a credit card or two. I was really careful not to get caught because I'd been back too often in too short a space of time.

Jim and I ended up going all over the place – Essex, Kent, Hertfordshire. And I would usually try to spend the money in department stores or high-street jewellers. They were the kind of shops I preferred mainly because I could get good suits in the department stores and jewellery sold on the high street wasn't so flash that it might arouse suspicion.

But I also went to just about anywhere else I thought I could get away with it. The main thing was to spend the limit in as few transactions as possible and then disappear.

When I didn't have any orders from anyone, or if I didn't need any suits, I'd go to other types of shops where, as it happened, I knew a lot of people.

And then I found other ways to spend the money. I'm naturally a chatty guy so often befriended shopkeepers, people who ran dealerships and service shops – places like MOT garages and tyre, carpet and DIY stores.

A lot of them, as it happened, were a bit corrupt, too.

Chip and PIN cards and machines weren't introduced to the UK until 2004. Before that, there was a manual system.

Embossed on the front of the credit card were the cardholder's name, address and unique identification number. When you went to pay for something, you gave the merchant your card and he/she put it face up on an 'imprinter' machine. A three-layer carbon paper was placed over the top of the card and an arm was drawn across the machine to take an imprint of the card details.

If the transaction was valuable, the shopkeeper would ring the credit card company to check that the card wasn't stolen. Of course, that could only have happened if the card owner had known that it had been nicked before it got to them. Which they never did.

You signed the top copy.

The merchant kept one copy, sent another to the credit card company and gave you the last one.

The process of getting the money from the company could take a few days depending on the postal service.

For someone committing fraud it was a doddle. There were no electronic or proper identity checks – you just went into a shop and came out with whatever you wanted.

I'd go in there and spend the limit. The card company would authorise it. So the business owner would be guaranteed their money no matter what happened.

The transaction would be for, let's say, a set of tyres, but I'd never take them from the shop so the shopkeeper could sell them to someone else and get the cash all over again.

We'd split the money 50-50, which meant I made quite a bit of cash on those days when I had a high-limit credit card.

The flow of cards from the postie wasn't that often, so there were still many days when I didn't have any cards to spend. Sometimes they dried up altogether – at which point, I went back to shoplifting.

And, in the end, I got caught, convicted and was sent to prison for credit card fraud. Thing was, though, it showed me that there were a lot of ways to make money.

I was always looking for new ways of doing things. Remember, I was only 18 at the time, only two years older than kids doing GCSEs, but I was an experienced thief, earning a few grand on some days by being a criminal. I'd been to young offenders a couple of times and was known to the local police and the local villains and gangsters.

As well as getting into credit cards, I adapted the way I stole from shops too. I still nicked stuff to order, but there was a way of getting cash back from the shops I'd robbed. Chain stores were good for this. You could rob a load of suits in a shop in Hertfordshire, damage them slightly – undo some of the stitching, break the zip or put a hole in one of the pockets – and then take the items back to a shop in the next town or county.

Nine times out of ten, I got my money back in cash. In those days, you didn't usually need a receipt and no one was that bothered about where you'd got them from.

By the end of the second day, I had £1200 in my pocket.

At the same time, I started to go for even higher-end shops to get the villains the suits they wanted.

They all loved a designer suit.

So I went into the big department stores in the West End and Regent Street for real top-of-the-range gear. Boss, Armani and all the rest of them.

Like my other scams, though, I had to think a bit creatively about how I did it.

These shops took shoplifting seriously – why wouldn't they? So much of the gear was really expensive.

All the suits had alarm tags on them and all the doors had security. Walking out with a bunch of suits and expecting to be able to leg it and escape wasn't going to work.

The alarms were like plastic tags made up of two halves fixed on either side of a bit of material. And each suit had two tags – one on the lapel and the other on the waistband of the trousers.

I don't know whether someone told me or if I worked it out, but it was a piece of piss to take the tags off: you just pushed a 2p piece under the lip of one half of the tag and bent it up. The tags fell away and you had a broken alarm and a £1000 suit.

The first day I went to a famous store, I was a bit nervous. I had an order for three suits from three of the villains at the pub. They were all slightly different sizes, which would be difficult to explain if someone asked.

Eventually, I went on to steal thousands of suits. Every villain and criminal in London has probably got one of those suits in their wardrobe!

I got so good at nicking to order that I could size someone just by looking at them: inside leg, waist and chest. To be honest, if I wasn't a drug addict, I could have opened a shop in Saville Row I was so accurate.

I had some Burton and Next bags to make it look as if I'd been out shopping for the day. I walked into the menswear section and picked four suits off the racks.

As soon as I pulled across the curtain in the changing room, I got to work on the alarms, putting the broken tags into the jacket pocket of the fourth suit. The one I didn't need.

Six alarms in all. I folded up the three suits I needed and put them into the shopping bags. As I walked out of the changing room, I put the fourth suit with all the alarm tags back on the rack.

Then I went up to the sports department and spent £50 on a tracksuit for myself, paid in cash, got the lift down to the ground floor and walked out through the busiest exit I could find.

It was that simple.

I charged the villains £350 per suit, which meant, including the money spent buying the tracksuit, I made a nice £1000 for not a very hard day's work.

It was such an easy routine that I managed to nick suits from all those top-end stores, and I don't think they were any the wiser until they carried out a stocktake. Remember, no CCTV or surveillance going on then. If you were really unlucky you might have been followed by a shop detective, but that was rare.

I felt so rich that I'd often get a minicab into the West End to do my robbing – it also helped if I got a bit nervous about being followed or someone shopping me to the police.

That night I walked into the pub and handed out the suits. It was a great feeling. I was the centre of attention.

Down the wine bar, all the gangsters, villains, car dealers and market stallholders were fitted out with designer suits provided by me.

I thought I was making a bit of a name for myself.

The pub was the focus of my life when I wasn't at Kay's with Joanne.

The gang was still very active and we'd meet up a lot, but we were up to different things now. Some of them were doing credit cards like me, some selling drugs and some were shoplifting. But we were all out grafting every day – just not together.

More often than not, when I walked into Fred's after I'd finished my work, the barmaid, Linda, would shout, 'Oi, Chubbsy, come and get your messages,' and then hand me a piece of paper – calls from the gang who wanted to know where I'd be later on that evening.

Fred would go mad at me. The gang all knew I'd be at the pub at some point in the evening, so they'd call and leave me messages to say if they were going to be in or if I should go off and meet them somewhere else.

'It's not your bleedin' office. Tell 'em to call your home.'

And then the phone would ring – really loudly – and he'd get even angrier.

'Chubbsy's Private Club. How can I help you?' he'd answer sarcastically before handing me the phone.

The nights in the pub were some of the best times of my life. I felt I belonged. There was great banter between all the guys. I was drinking and enjoying myself. I felt I was getting closer to being the kind of guys I used to see coming into The Cricketers when my dad was a landlord.

I was earning good money from something that wasn't too risky – not that the risk ever really bothered me – and I felt my standing was rising all the time with the gangsters and villains I looked up to and wanted to emulate.

By the time I was looking at my 19th birthday, I thought I was pretty well set up and that this would be my life.

I was totally involved in crime every day along with drinking and taking drugs.

One Saturday after I'd been drinking all day, I decided to go to the Indian restaurant just around the corner. I was obliterated but sat in there for a good two hours eating vindaloos, naan breads, onion bhajis and washing it all down with a couple of bottles of wine.

Around 8 p.m., I was ready for another session and decided I wanted some ecstasy. I called the local dealer who dropped off three pills. Leaving the restaurant, I necked all three and made my way to the wine bar.

Within a minute or so, I was violently sick down the alleyway, which was nothing uncommon. But within another five minutes, I was at the bar ordering a large vodka and looking forward to the rest of my evening.

About 40 minutes later, the ecstasy had not kicked in. Normally, it'd be coming on after 20 minutes, but I realised that I must have thrown them up in the alleyway with the curry and wine.

I got straight back on the phone to order more pills, but the dealer said that he'd sold out. I was gutted. But I had an idea. I left the bar, went down the alley to where I'd been sick and dug out the three half-digested pills and swallowed them. Again.

Over the next five to six hours, there I was out of my head, detached from society, not caring about anyone or anything apart from myself and thinking that I was OK! But I wasn't. Addiction had got me.

Not surprisingly, Joanne was getting fed up with me. I spent so much time out doing credit cards or shoplifting and every evening at the pub that she never saw me.

The instability of my lifestyle and the potential for getting picked up by the police weighed on her, too. Her idea of what a relationship should be like was nothing like this.

More and more often, I'd have to sneak out of the pub or tell the barmaid not to tell her where I was if she called. Sometimes she'd come to the pub and drag me home.

In the mornings before she went to work, she'd make me promise not to go, but when it came to pub time, I'd just go anyway. The physical calling of the alcohol and drugs was too much. It was just too tempting.

The villains in the pub were all in their 50s, but they liked my energy and I was entertaining. They took me to clubs like Hollywood's in Romford. As soon as I got there with them, the bouncers would wave us all in. Any time after that when I turned up by myself or with my gang, the bouncers recognised me as being a mate of the villains. I never had to queue again.

So it was another part of life where I thought I was winning. My standing seemed to be going up in the area and I loved it. Being recognised like that was just the kind of attention I wanted. My ego was going through the roof. I thought I had arrived.

The fact that Joanne was getting fed up didn't bother me particularly, apart from the fact that it was annoying to have a voice telling me or pleading with me not to go out all the time.

But she didn't give up. By this time I'd been doing it for a year and my 19th birthday was approaching. She gave me an ultimatum.

'Come on, just leave the gang, stop the crime, get a job. We can settle down. I don't want the police here all the time. And I don't want to worry all the time that you've been nicked or stabbed.'

I don't know why, but I agreed. Whether it was just to stop her nagging me or whether I just thought I should. It didn't matter in the end.

It turned out that Big D's uncle owned a scaffolding business, and he got me a job.

I stopped the credit cards, the shoplifting, the pub every night. But I still went out a lot with the scaffolders – and tried to be a bit more 'normal'. I still hung out with the gang when I could.

But it was a pain – getting up early every morning, working physically hard every day and with regular hours. And, to be really honest, it was so boring. So boring. There was no adrenalin rush at work – you didn't have to plan anything or work anything out. And, to top it all, the money was shit.

It worked for about six months.

One Monday morning, the alarm went off at 6 a.m. as usual and I just thought, 'Sod it.' I turned over and went back to sleep.

The next day, I got a new batch of credit cards and went off with Jewish Jim on the rob. I felt alive again.

At 19, then, I was living in a big house and had a girlfriend; I was making great money, thanks to going back to my old ways, and getting a reputation with the local villains and gangsters. More than anything, though, I was really happy. Life felt good, and I couldn't imagine myself doing anything different than what I was doing – for the rest of my life.

And I felt like I was probably the most trusted and most popular in the gang. I'd had two stretches in young offenders, was good at shoplifting and the credit card scam, and my local pub, the place where I hung out with villains and gangsters, was now the place where we met.

It was, as Fred hated to call it, my office. I really felt like I was a leader and I absolutely loved it. Life was sweet. I didn't know then, but I do now, that the illness which would take me a millimetre away from death had got a grip on me already.

CHAPTER EIGHT

Doing the amount of crime I was doing meant that I got nicked every now and again.

And now that I was over 18, this meant adult prison. I had a good few stretches in Brixton, Wormwood Scrubs, Chelmsford and Pentonville over the next couple of years.

When you get nicked in a place in London, you get sent to a certain prison. It works a bit like a school catchment area.

They were all very different places despite the fact that the routines were almost exactly the same.

Back in the 90s, they called Brixton Prison a 'shithole' for a reason. It stank of shit, piss and BO. I gagged the first time I walked in there.

It was bottom of the government's league tables and everything about it was humiliating. Even the inspector of prisons at the time called it a 'hellhole'.

Because they were so short-staffed, the guards would lock us up for 23 hours a day.

There were no toilets in the cells, so you had to have a shit on a piece of newspaper, fold it up and throw it out of the window. The windows had bars that you had to aim through. There was no curtain or privacy, so you had to do it in front of your cellmate. We usually waited till it was dark so at least we weren't in full view of each other.

And then, the next morning, this is absolutely true, a prisoner who had the job of 'poo collector' would walk around the outside of the buildings with a huge black bucket picking up the shit parcels from hundreds of cells. He got £20 a week for that. More than the average wage – but still, he was picking up hundreds of packets of shit. Who would want to do that?

When we were let out of our cells for an hour, the rush to use the toilets was mad. Within 10 minutes, the toilets were blocked and you couldn't use them. There was shit all over the floor.

Over the couple of years while I was doing all right with the shoplifting and credit cards, I ended up in Brixton twice, but my first male adult prison sentence was at Wormwood Scrubs. They got me on shoplifting and handling stolen goods. Five months. I was just 20 at the time.

The days were always the same. And the same in most prisons I was in too.

A prison day went like this:

The doors were unlocked at about 7 a.m. every morning, and in those days you had to slop out – there was a bucket in each cell for you to piss in. You had to queue up every morning and pour the piss down the drain before breakfast.

If you needed to have a shit, as mentioned already, then you used the newspaper. It was against a 'prisoners' code' to shit in the bucket – it'd stay there all night stinking out the cell. So you'd use the newspaper and chuck it out of the window.

Then you went down for breakfast, which consisted of porridge, an egg and some hot water to make tea. Usually you had to take the food back to your cell, so you'd be locked up while the guards had their breakfast.

The guy I was first twinned with was called, let's say, Bob. He was doing 14 years for armed robbery. He was a fit, athletic guy and we got on OK. That wasn't always the case: in Brixton I got to share with an old alcoholic who'd shit himself and talk to himself all the time.

Bob was on a recall, meaning that he'd got out, done another armed robbery and got caught. He was sent back down with an increased sentence. Reoffenders were all over the prison – there were so many people who'd got out and come straight back in.

When I'd gone into the prison, they'd put me on landing five on the works wing. Everyone on that wing had a job. Mine was in the laundry, which was a pretty cushy number because you had all the brand-new clean stuff coming through: boxers, trousers, overalls, socks.

The old stuff we had to wash had been knocking around for a few years and was disgusting.

You took what you wanted for yourself and you could do mates favours as well. You had a really good kit.

I had to feed the sheets through the tumble driers and then through heated rollers. It pressed and dried them at the same time.

So after breakfast, I'd be taken to the laundry to start my day's work. The morning shift ended about 12 p.m. when I was taken for my lunch. Again, I'd collect the sandwich and teabag and go back up to the cell. We were locked in again for another hour or hour and a half while the screws had their lunch.

We slopped out and then went back to work.

The afternoon shift was usually easier because if you worked hard in the morning, you'd finish quite early and could sit around, have a cup of tea and chat.

By 5 p.m. you were taken back to your landing and could have a shower.

Sometimes there were fights and threats, but mainly people just got on with it and each other. I kept my head down, obeyed the rules and didn't bother anyone.

You looked out for people on your wing too; there was a good spirit mainly among the prisoners. The staff treated us like adults, which we were, but it meant there was no 'Yes, sir' or 'No, sir' like in the young offenders places. I think the screws in adult prison had less ego than the ones in the juvenile places who probably still had a bit of self-respect.

The screws didn't mess with you unless you misbehaved, and then they'd give you a beating; but if you were all right and did what you were supposed to do, it was OK.

About 5.30 p.m. you got your tea. It depended on how many staff they had, but usually they put you in lockdown till 7 p.m. when you were opened up again for association. Again, it all depended on staff numbers. Brixton was the worst place because the staff never lasted long and they were always short, so we were locked up most of the day.

Association, if it was allowed, would be till 8.30 p.m. when you went back to the cell. It was the time when you could play pool, table tennis and watch TV. Some nights they put on film nights. But in general, it was a time you could mix – so you could go in other cells and have a brew and a chat or play some cards. All the cell doors were open and you could go to different landings.

It was also the time when everyone did their little drug deals or you'd go and have a slug of the hooch someone had been brewing. Disgusting stuff, but you'd do anything to get a bit of a kick or a buzz.

Mars bars and cigarettes back then were the main currency. So you'd swap a few Mars bars for a bit of hooch or some cannabis.

I was a pretty good pool player – from growing up in the pub – so I used to play for Mars bars and then I'd eat them. I hadn't taken heroin at that point, but I smoked a bit of cannabis that my cellmate got in. The prison was full of cannabis.

Then at about 8.30 you had to go back to your cell. The door was locked, but the flap stayed open so the screws could do a roll-call to make sure everyone was accounted for.

They'd come around with a clipboard and the list of who was in which cell, call your name out and you'd stand in front of the flap so they could see you. Your name was ticked off, the flap was closed and that was it for the day.

That was the regime at Wormwood Scrubs. I didn't find it too bad, and to be honest I preferred it to young offenders because you had more freedom and the screws weren't on your case the whole time. And you did get out of your cell unless there was trouble going on or they were really short-staffed.

And it wasn't as if I was ever there for a long stretch. Six months maximum usually, and that went pretty quickly.

But Brixton was different. It was disgusting. I used to hate it if I was nicked in the catchment area for that place, as I knew it would be horrendous. That first time, though, I was there for about six weeks after I got nicked in Harrods for trying to rob £2000 worth of Ralph Lauren shirts.

It wasn't just the smell as soon as you were marched in, and the fact that the place was falling apart, the food was disgusting and there were so many prisoners in there with very serious mental health problems.

Really, really bad problems. There were people with terrible addictions, schizophrenia, extreme paranoia and a lot on suicide watch.

And there were never enough staff, so you were in lockdown 23 hours a day. Just trapped in your cell with whoever you'd been thrown in with. The first time was with that guy 'Bob'.

Some of the stuff I saw in Brixton still haunts me, and I've seen some very, very bad things in my time in the crack dens. I think what

I saw back then is a bit more like what prison life really is even now. With the arrival of spice and so much heroin in prisons, the amount of self-harm and suicide is going through the roof.

Last year (2019) there was a 37% rise in prison suicides, but the government doesn't even know how many were drug related. What they do know, though, is that since 2010, 80,000 years of prison officer experience has been lost from the prison service. This means that there are masses of inexperienced screws walking around not knowing what to do in the case of emergencies. Most of them have less than two years' experience, so when they find somebody who is having a mental health crisis or appears to be dying, they are unsure whether to just raise the alarm or go into the cell.

What I saw back in the 90s was terrible, though – even with experienced screws.

The worst thing you could do in prison was get into debt. If that happened, there was nowhere to hide. I knew a guy – a really nice guy – called Lloyd. I met him in Pentonville and then again in Brixton.

Lloyd liked to smoke a bit of heroin but didn't really bother anyone. Unfortunately, he got in with a bad crowd and owed this one guy – a nasty piece of work – some money. Nothing much – a £20 heroin debt is what I heard. This guy paid someone to cut him.

I was coming back from exercise one day and went past his cell. There was blood everywhere. I mean, you could have had a good paddle in the cell there was so much on the floor. And the walls and ceiling were all spattered with it, too.

It was a real mess. What had happened was the guy had taken the lid off a tin of baked beans, sharpened it on the wall outside Lloyd's cell and then gone in and set about him.

He'd cut him deep from his jawline to the top of his eye. It was the most horrific scar you'll ever see. The helicopter ambulance came and got him and took him to hospital. They said he had 450 stitches to his face, both inside and outside.

In prison if you get into debt, you're in trouble. There's nowhere to hide and the screws aren't going to protect you. It's not the guards who run the prison; it's the prisoners. If you get into debt with the wrong people – and usually they're the ones lending the money in the first place – then you're in for a beating. Just like Lloyd.

Prison came with the territory. You do crime; you get nicked. My life carried on with the gang, the pub, Joanne and her mum. It was still my daily way of life, but it was about to turn very, very sour.

CHAPTER NINE

Jon, another gang member, got a prison sentence for something or other. I can't remember and it doesn't really matter. He got three months but turned up at the pub after a month.

When he got out, we went off to Norwich to do some shoplifting. But we got greedy and were nicked by some shop detectives.

Bad news. He was looking at going back inside almost straight away. We were kept in Norwich police station for ages – at least six or seven hours – while they processed us.

So it was really late when we got back to Essex. All the pubs were closed, but I wanted to get a drink and get stoned – put the day behind me by getting wasted. I was pissed off.

A ring around the usual dealers got us nowhere. Either no one had anything or they didn't pick up the phone. I was getting really down and angry.

At the time, Jon was living over on the Thames View Estate, Barking, with his mum. His mum wasn't there much because she had a new boyfriend and she stayed at his a lot. Jon had the flat to himself most of the time.

We headed back there to see if his mum had any booze in. Anything really – I just wanted to get something down me to take the edge off the day. And when you're that age, you have to have things immediately.

We were turning out the cupboards and the sideboard but couldn't find anything.

As I slammed the last cupboard door shut, Jon looked at me. He looked serious.

'Paul, I've got something to tell you.'

'What? Have you got a secret cannabis stash somewhere? Come on, out with it.' I tried to make a joke of it hoping that he really did have some drugs somewhere.

'When I was in jail last month, I tried heroin.'

'You bastard.' I looked at him in complete disgust and said, 'Why the hell did you want to take that rubbish?'

When I think about it now, it was an absolutely massive moment in my life.

Growing up, whenever I saw heroin addicts I just thought 'scumbags'. To me and the rest of the gang, they were just the lowest of the low. They were filthy, had no self-respect and stank. They were the opposite of what I wanted to be. I was sharp, well-dressed – they looked like tramps. They had no money and no life.

It was almost a rule of the gang, a bit like carrying a knife, that none of us did heroin. We hated anyone who did.

So if there was one thing I didn't want to be, it was a heroin addict.

'What do you mean you tried heroin? You must be mad. How many times?'

'Yeah, I was locked up with this geezer who took it. Tried it two or three times. Tell you what, it was lovely.'

'Don't give a shit how lovely it was. I don't want anything to do with it. You can piss off.'

I went to leave the flat, but he'd found some vodka in one of the kitchen cupboards, so I stuck around for a bit. If only I'd left there and then.

About half an hour later, after we'd finished the vodka, he turned to me again and said, 'There's a guy upstairs who sells it. Shall we get some?'

'Sells what?'

'Heroin.'

'No. I don't want it. Let's try and get some alcohol and weed.'

We rang around, but there was still no one with anything. We were stuck without anything after a shit day.

So I just thought, 'Sod it. Let's just get twenty pounds' worth of heroin.'

We bought two £10 bags.

I was scared.

The picture is still so clear in my mind. Jon got tinfoil and a lighter.

He tore off a strip of foil and rolled it into a tube – a bit like a joint. Then he tore off another small bit and made a square a couple of centimetres across.

He took one of the £10 bags of brown powder and tipped some on the square piece of foil. I can still see his hands shaking as he lifted the tube up to his lips.

Jon put the tube in his mouth, picked up the foil square with the heroin on it with his left hand and got the lighter in his right.

He looked up at me as he flicked the lighter and the flame sparked. Still looking at me, he moved it under the foil when his eyes moved back down to watch the heroin heat up.

Seconds later, a white smoke started to rise up from the foil. He put the lighter down and used his right hand to guide the tube – still in his mouth – towards the smoke.

He inhaled.

Then he chased a bit more of the smoke as it snaked upwards.

He inhaled.

Chasing the dragon.

I watched with sweaty palms.

I thought about all the times I'd looked at heroin users with disgust. Lowlife.

I thought about how many conversations I'd had with the gang about what utter scum smackheads were. And how none of us would ever do it.

I thought about Joanne and her mum and my mum, and how worried Joanne was about my drinking and smoking.

Then I watched Jon's face when he took the last pull on the smoke. He put the tube and square on the table and sat back.

He grinned at me. And then did another line.

'Go on then, give me a few drags.'

Those eight words nearly killed me.

I sat up straight, almost bracing myself for what was about to happen.

I put the tube in my mouth as Jon flicked the lighter. The flame appeared and then disappeared under the foil.

In my memory, my eyes seemed to sharpen their focus as I looked down on the white powder slowly turning brown.

Then the smoke appeared.

I looked at it for a moment. Pausing, not sure that this was something I should do, but not being able to resist the temptation of doing something so bad.

'Go on,' he said.

I sucked the smoke in hard, moving my head up to chase it, hoovering up every last trace.

I put the tube down on the table and sat back on the sofa.

Nothing.

I felt absolutely nothing.

All the tension came exploding out of me.

'Where does that prick live? I'll throttle him. He's sold us some rubbish. I want my money back.'

Jon just made a 'calm' movement with his hand, like he was stroking a cat or something. He sat back and closed his eyes.

Then it hit me.

Bang. I couldn't move. Paralysed. The feeling of total bliss running through my blood. The tingling, buzzing, beautiful feeling of a total pure high.

People talk about the euphoria of heroin. The total ecstasy of the high you get from it.

I thought I was actually in Heaven, but I had no idea I was at the Gates of Hell and on the verge of a lifelong battle with misery and addiction. I had never ever felt anything like it before.

My mind was blown – I hadn't expected that it would feel like this. This drug took me to a different level – miles above alcohol or ecstasy.

First, there was the incredible rush – a surge of pure physical pleasure – that almost knocked you over it was so powerful.

And then, as that slowed down, there was an incredible state of almost like being in a dream. Everything seemed to slow down, be soft and gentle; I couldn't help just smiling all the way through.

It was like a combination of ecstasy and tripping on acid combined with the total stoned feeling of smoking a load of really great quality cannabis. It takes all fear. You are just in that moment of total high – it takes you to a place of nothing. There's no yesterday, tomorrow or anything except that moment.

We sat in his mum's flat overlooking the Thames. Jon put on a UB40 CD as the outside lights and the lights from the barges going up and down the river caught the water. There were reflections and shadows, sparkling effects against the darkness – it was all magical.

But it was a sucker punch. Nothing that amazing comes for free.

I thought that night I was in Heaven, but this drug was so powerful that for the next 15 years it manipulated and controlled every moment and minute of my life. I was now standing at the Gates of Hell.

The next morning I woke up. But actually, I think I had just came out of the trance I was in. I don't think I slept much at all. I said, 'Jesus, Jon, we've got to keep this quiet. Don't say nothing. To anyone.'

I knew Big D and the others would be raging with anger.

And I felt really, really ashamed that I'd tried it.

I left the flat and went home.

I went back to my life. Grafting, doing the credit cards, going to the pub, seeing my mates in the gang.

But something had changed. The high, the rush I got from heroin was like a voice whispering in the back of my head. It was calling me back all the time. When I took a sip of lager or had a pull on a joint, the voice was saying, 'It's not as good as heroin.'

It seemed to take the enjoyment out of the high I was getting because I knew there was something 1000 times better.

I felt as though I'd opened a door I couldn't close.

A couple of days went by.

I was out with Jon again grafting in Bluewater. We'd got away with a load of stuff, fenced it and then went back to his.

'Do you want to get some more?'

'Yes.'

Me, aged 2, already obsessed with football

The only picture I could find of Joanne and me (aged 20)

Me (far right) with the boys at Hollywood night club 1990 (aged 21)

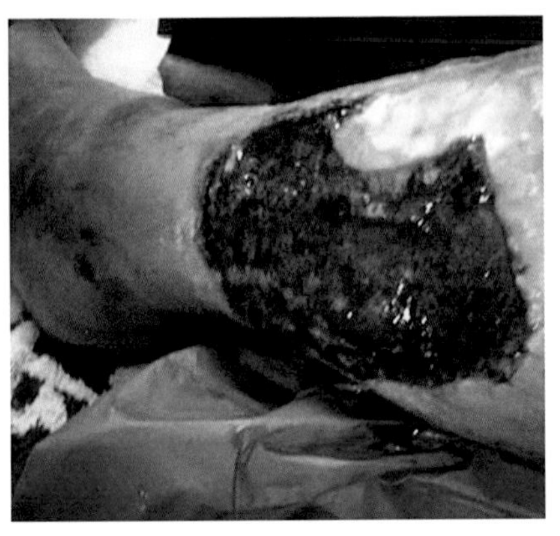

A picture taken by doctors before one of the many operations to fix my damaged legs

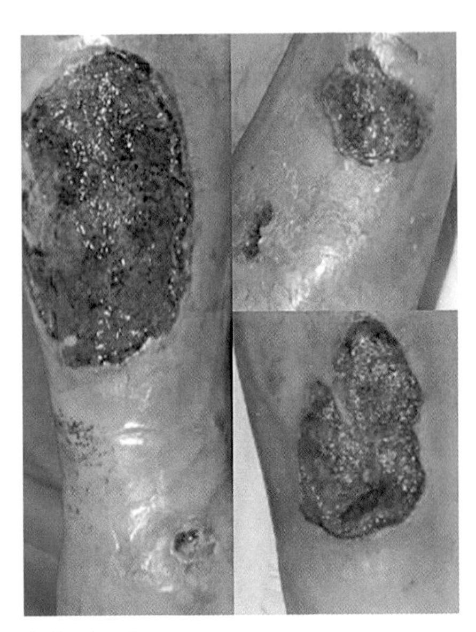

Both of my legs

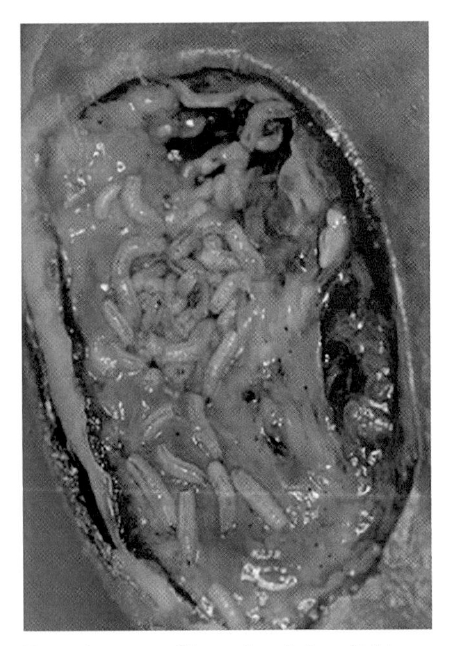

Maggots were put in my legs in hospital to eat away the infection and rotten tissue

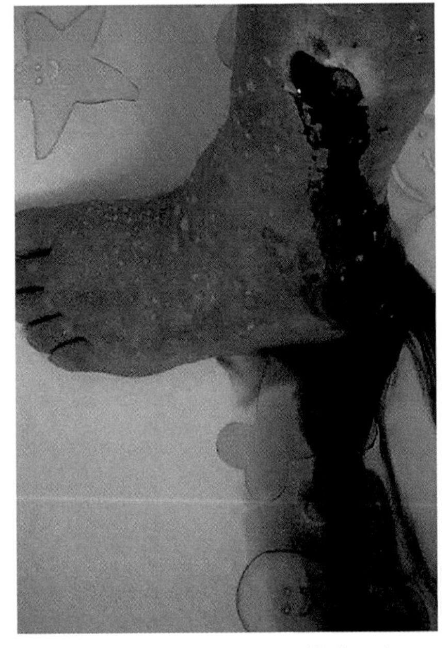

My legs still bleed after years of being clean

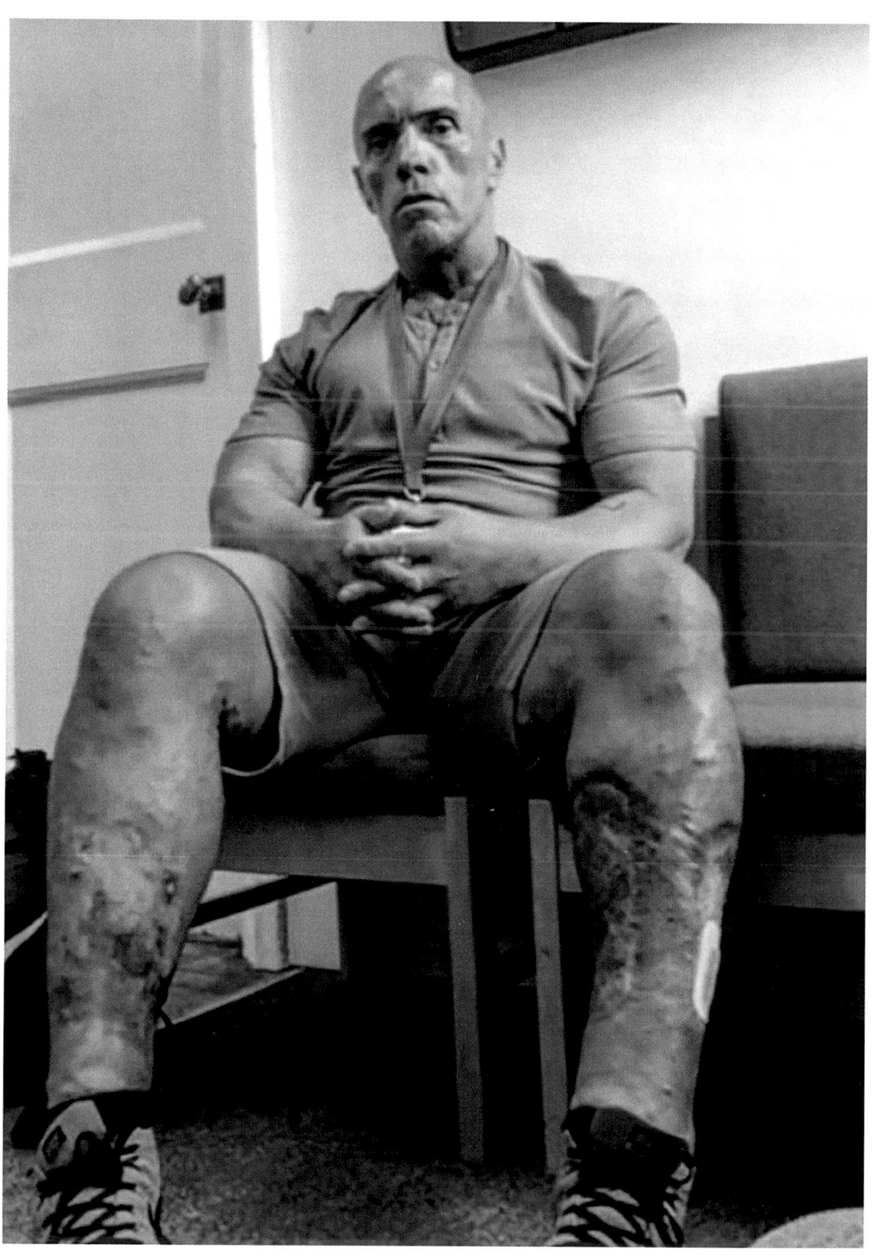

In a Hertfordshire school reception, waiting to give an assembly to hundreds of pupils

Year 9 assembly in Yorkshire, giving a talk on drugs and knife crime

Year 8 assembly on addiction and gangs

Years 4,5 and 6 assembly in Charlton, London

Year 9 assembly in London, giving a talk on gangs, alcoholism and drugs

Year 11 assembly in Cumbria

Educating 6–10 year-old Cub Scouts and Beavers in Essex

At a primary school in Somerset giving a talk on drugs, alcohol and gangs

One of the perks of my job is when schools have dogs on site for pupils' Social, emotional and mental health (SEMH) needs

My favourite place, feeding the horses

Talk in East London with some young lads from the Kicks football programme

Year 10 assembly London

Just after a workshop with doctors from the London HEMS (Helicopter Emergency Medical Service) team about knife and gun crime

In London giving the police a workshop on the true nature and consequences of drug addiction and alcoholism

In Brighton, at a trauma conference giving a lecture on drug addiction and alcoholism to senior doctors, nurses, and paramedics

With the London Fire Brigade LIFE course about to go in to HMP Feltham Young Offenders to do a reoffending reduction workshop

Wembley Fire Station giving a talk on their LIFE course with some local school kids

Me and my dear mum in Romford market as she met up with me to give me my birthday card

Me and my wonderful daughter, Ria, out for a cheeky Nando's for my birthday

Me and my mum at a cafe in Essex on my 50th birthday

My dad who I never really got to know. I will always cherish the few years he was in my life and I hope God's taking care of him 🙏🖤

CHAPTER TEN

The thing about heroin is that it acts quite quickly on your body – if you smoke it, it'll hit you after 10 or 15 seconds.

The rush of the first high is incredible, and then you're spaced out, relaxed, chilled and out of it for hours.

After the first couple of lines, I was obsessed. It's a bit like when I was a kid and wanted to play out on the street – chasing that rush is just about the only thing on my mind.

Me and Jon went out robbing every day, and the heroin started to become more and more regular. I was spending more and more time at his mum's place.

Joanne and Kay knew something was up, but I wouldn't tell them what it was.

The gang started to call me on my mobile – this technology had just come out and I got a mobile phone straight away – trying to find me, but I didn't always pick up. I'd go for days without seeing anyone but Jon.

The thing about heroin is that it draws you in very quickly.

It didn't take long, just a few months, for me to start losing weight. Remember, I was a happy 18-stone lump who was immaculately dressed. Within five months, I had lost two stone and there were the first brown marks on my usually immaculate white teeth.

My clothes were starting to hang off me a bit and, to be honest, I wasn't that bothered about how I looked any more.

And this is the moment when the descent into Hell really starts.

From being an energetic, social, perhaps a bit of a naughty bloke who bent the rules and lived on just the wrong side of the law, I started to withdraw.

My focus was already starting to narrow so that I was thinking more and more about when I could next do heroin – so I didn't see the gang very much and even when I did, I was itching to get away so I could smoke some more.

One night I was out with the gang in the pub. I went to the toilet cubicle to have a quick smoke of heroin and Charlie came in – he'd joined quite recently. The gang, apart from the core members, chopped and changed a bit overtime. He recognised the smell because he once knew someone who had started doing it a few years previously. He confronted me. I denied it, but he knew. And he told me he knew.

When I went back into the pub, he called me out in front of all the others. There was a massive row. Big D and Wilson were furious. They were so angry that I thought they were going to kill me. Charlie pulled out his knife, held it in front of my face and said, 'Whoever got you on that shit, I'm going to open them up.'

I knew he was serious because I'd seen him do it many times before. Wilson and Big D held him back.

When it came out that it was Jon who'd got me into it, they wanted to crucify him. Tear him to bits.

That was the beginning of the end of the gang. These boys or young men had become like brothers to me, but it was coming to an end. This brown powder (heroin) took me to a very dark place. But the terrible thing was that I didn't really care.

We'd been together every day for seven years, and I'd just let it go. I wasn't interested in them or having a laugh or going to the pub. All of the stuff that had been important to me, the reputation I was so happy to get going in Romford, the pride I got from becoming a man and doing stuff – even if it was robbing and crime – didn't count for anything. All I wanted was the next hit of heroin.

Within a year, I'd lost five stone. The green and brown colour on my teeth was spreading from smoking. My world had narrowed to one word: heroin.

About a year after I'd taken my first hit, I was with this addict called Mark in Barking. We had just scored some heroin and gone back to his place.

He injected. I'd heard from loads of people that it was a much sweeter hit than smoking. So I used one of his clean needles, and he showed me what to do.

You have to mix the heroin powder with some liquid to be able to get it into the syringe. We used citric acid – because it breaks down the heroin – and water. So you put the powder on a spoon and add the liquid.

Then you heat it up with a lighter from underneath until the mixture becomes liquid.

Mark then put a cigarette filter on the spoon to soak up all the liquid – the idea was that it took out any impurities.

You put the needle in the filter, draw up the liquid and inject into your arm.

Once you've found the vein, you put the needle in, push the liquid in slowly and then sit back.

And that was it. I never smoked heroin again. Injecting it was an immediate, massive rush.

Before long, Joanne and Kay were finding bloody needles and syringes in the laundry basket from whenever I stayed. As well as bloodstained pants and T-shirts in the washing and in the bathroom where I used to inject.

They knew what I was up to and were desperate for me to get off it.

Joanne was always saying, 'Please, Paul, just get on a rehab programme, get away from it.'

I did try once. Cleaned myself up. Got sober. Tried to live the 'normal' life – just as I had before heroin. But I couldn't handle it. I relapsed and went back out with Jon. Nothing could compete with the power of the drug.

Everything in my life was falling away, yet I couldn't do anything to stop it. I knew this wasn't the life I wanted but was terrified of not being high or drunk. The addiction had me and wasn't going to let me go.

After six months, I gave up trying to stay at Joanne's. It was too much for everyone, and I didn't have the freedom I wanted to go out and get wasted every day.

Jon and I went out every day – nicking, fencing and injecting. He was a full-blown addict, too, and both of us just lived for heroin.

Six months later – when I was 22 – I discovered crack cocaine.

If that first smoke of heroin with Jon was the start of my journey to Hell, finding crack and using it was like seeing the bottom of the pit of Hell and deciding to go and live in it.

It was the start of 15 years of total misery. The whole point of writing this book is to show people that the disease of addiction is clever and relentless. It sneaks up on you and once it's got a hold, it won't let you go. The junkie's life consists of only one thing: getting the next hit.

After I'd started on the heroin, three of the gang started, too. Within 12 years, they had all died of overdoses.

Another four of them are tramping around London with terrible mental health, rotten teeth, filthy dirty and begging for money.

All of them were healthy before they started – two of them could have gone on to be professional footballers.

Out of all the gang and the many hundreds of other addicts I met on my journey, I think I'm the only one who came out of it and went on to do something positive with my life. What a waste of so many lives.

CHAPTER ELEVEN

All the drugs I took were terrible, but with crack cocaine I couldn't switch off – I just sat for days taking it.

Even smoking it gives you the most incredible rush – a buzz like you'll never get from anything else. The high lasts maybe 5 or 10 minutes.

But then the crash comes and it is so, so bad. It's as if your body does the exact opposite of what the high gave you.

And you're just left with the voice in your head shouting that you have to have more. And more. Crack is the ultimate addiction, and getting out of it is a complete nightmare.

When it comes out of Columbia, the cocaine is 95% pure. But by the time it gets onto the streets of London, it's gone through 10 pairs of hands and been cut with all sorts of shit. So the 95% pure cocaine is now 20%. To turn the cocaine back into more pure or crack cocaine, you do freebasing, which is when you put it on a spoon and add water and bicarbonate of soda or ammonia. When you heat it up in a spoon, all the additives evaporate and you're left with pure cocaine. You leave it to go hard, to turn into a rock, and then you can smoke or inject it.

Heroin was bad, but this was much, much worse.

I was already injecting a lot of heroin – my habit was about £100 a day.

To buy the drugs, I'd be out with Jon robbing suits, alcohol, cigarettes. We'd do our normal routine of going to the department stores to see what we could get. We'd sometimes go high-end to get better quality stuff, but the daily grind was just an activity to get enough to buy the heroin.

He had a car, no tax or MOT, but it was easier to get away with that stuff back then, and we'd go to the shopping centres and rob our stuff.

But when I started taking crack, my daily spend was more like £400-£500. My fences used to give me 25% of the value of the goods, so I had to nick £1600-£2000 worth of stuff every day just to feed and maintain my drug taking for one day.

That's a lot of robbing. That's a lot of running out of shops. That's a lot of driving to different shopping malls to try somewhere new.

It was a full-time job. I was being totally controlled by this illness.

And then, because I can never stop once I've got on to something new, I started to inject crack cocaine.

If you ask any doctor, they'll tell you that this is the worst thing you can do. For the 5- or 10-minute high, it is unreal. The rush is just amazing. But it gives you a lifetime of problems and pain.

Injecting crack is a bit like injecting heroin – you need to heat it up to get rid of the impurities that the dealers cut the drugs with. They'll put ammonia or bicarbonate of soda in the mix just to bulk up the product.

Heating it will get rid of all that crap and you're left with pure crack.

I used the heroin to counteract the effects of coming down off the crack hit. As I injected more crack, I needed more heroin to be able to deal with the comedown. There's no easy way out of that spiral.

When you start to inject crack, you're basically putting your body in massive danger.

Your veins start to harden and thrombose. This causes two problems: Injecting into the vein becomes much more difficult especially if you have abscesses in the groin, which I did. The wall you're trying to break with the needle is harder, so you have to push with more force, and sometimes you break a needle. And you start to develop clots, as the blood can't flow through the veins as easily.

Because your focus is 100% getting high, you don't eat, wash, sleep; you start to hear and see things. You get paranoid very quickly and acutely.

But none of that matters because you're just chasing the next hit.

My weight dropped so dramatically, I ended up at 8½ stone. That from being a lump of 18 stone just a few years previously.

When I was out and about in Romford, I'd bump into people I knew, but they wouldn't recognise me.

The gang still knew who I was, but there was a problem. I was walking down Romford High Street one night with a couple of other heroin addicts.

We walked past a pub, it was dark, and it seemed like the street was a bit quiet. Suddenly, everything exploded with noise and movement.

I looked around and the other two addicts were lying on the floor, unconscious, their faces flowing with blood, their bodies twitching and battered.

Three of the gang had spotted me, piled out of the pub, beaten these two addicts senseless and then gone back in and carried on drinking. They never made eye contact with me at any point during or after it happened.

They didn't touch me but were so angry about what heroin had done to me that they kicked the addicts until they were knocked out.

That created a problem for me with other addicts because they knew that if the gang saw me with heroin users, the gang would beat them up. Other addicts started to avoid hanging around with me.

But the real shock came when I was walking along the high street, past all the old places – Kentucky, the off-licence, Debenhams. I looked up from my normal staring at the pavement walk and saw my mum coming towards me.

She was only five or six yards away. She caught my eye but looked right through me. Like I wasn't there.

She hadn't recognised me. A mum who didn't recognise her own son.

That's how unwell I looked.

As it happens, though, I was nervous about seeing her because not long before, when my normal sources of income weren't there – I think maybe Jon's car was off the road or something – I ended up breaking into her house and stealing her jewellery, including her wedding ring, Nottingham Bob's tools and my brothers' Xboxes and PlayStations. I cleaned the place out just to get money for drugs.

That's how low I went because of the illness of drug and alcohol addiction. From a cheerful, bubbly, energetic 10-year-old who loved his family, I was now robbing from them.

It's one of the things I was most ashamed of when I started rehab.

In less than two years I'd become this absolute mess of a junkie – exactly the person I used to despise on the street. I never changed my clothes, but was either out grafting or injecting.

If Jon hadn't had a place, I would have been a homeless lowlife crack and heroin addict.

But drug addicts don't have any loyalty to anything except the next fix. And dealers don't care about anything except selling their gear and making as much money as possible.

When I rang to buy, they'd say, 'Meet me in five, ten minutes at the station.' So I'd turn up at the meeting place. Usually they've told two or three more addicts the same thing. Selling to more than one person at a time obviously makes sense because it reduces the risk of getting spotted or caught. And it increases their profits because they only have to make one journey.

But they treated us like dirt on the sole of their shoe. An hour later, we could all still be hanging about waiting. And the dealers know we're in a desperate state. Terrified of withdrawing and standing around for ages – in winter, freezing cold on street corners, shivering – and waiting.

Finally, a dealer would turn up. A new BMW or some huge 4x4 Range Rover gliding to a halt near to us. The window would be wound down just two or three inches – enough for me and the other addicts to pass the money through and take the drugs. As I reached in my hand, in winter, I could feel the heat of the car. It was torture.

As soon as the deal was done, the car would take off and I'd head straight to the nearest public toilets or fast-food restaurant so I could inject. I spent hours in those places while the dealers went back to their warm, expensive, secure and comfortable houses, everything bought using the money the suffering addicts got from stealing. I paid them millions over the years. They didn't care. It was business for them and they treated us like vermin.

Jon and I started to drift apart as I met other addicts. Usually while I was waiting and we got chatting. This new junkie might say he knew a place around the corner, so we'd go off there to get our first hit.

And that was it. I could stay for two nights or two weeks. Drug dens don't have tenancy agreements; you move on when you want to or when you get kicked out.

In theory, I could stay in 10 different crack dens in two weeks in 10 different towns. And all that time I never changed my clothes, brushed my teeth or had any kind of wash. I was a stinking wreck of a man.

On one of these deals I met a guy I'll call Little Peter. He had a place in Romford and sold cannabis and heroin.

There was one other guy, Ian.

And then this quite smart bloke called Lal started appearing.

Lal had a big house somewhere else in Essex. On the face of it, he looked quite healthy. Much better than the rest of us for sure.

He liked a bit of nice gear – clothes, shoes and stuff – to look the part of a successful person. He had a car so he'd take me out shoplifting. We'd do all the usual places, but now I had proper wheels and a mate looking out for me.

Every morning Lal would pick me up from Peter's and we'd head off to a shopping centre or town somewhere and I'd go robbing – paying him in cash and clothes for the transport.

Then we'd get our gear and head back to Peter's to inject.

For nearly 10 years this was my daily routine.

But the injecting started to take an even greater toll on my body. As my veins hardened, I started to get infections.

Then one day at Lal's house, I injected with a needle I'd used too many times. As I pulled it out of the hard vein, it snapped off. The tip was buried in my arm.

'Lal, my needle's snapped. Got any tweezers?'

He handed me some tweezers, and I dug around for ages trying to get the metal out. Blood was shooting everywhere but I just succeeded in pushing the needle further in.

At that point, I just thought sod it and gave up. I just didn't think about what might happen and I really didn't care. I wanted a fresh needle and another hit.

So I left the needle in there.

Three days later, my arm blew up. It was infected – my bicep was the size of a basketball.

I went to A&E. The doctor took one look at me and said he'd do an X-ray. When the picture came back, he saw a needle in my arm.

'You're crazy. I can't believe you left it in there. You should have come straight away. Why didn't you?'

'I couldn't. I had to get drugs.'

The only reason I went to hospital was because I had a pocket full of drugs – I knew they were going to keep me in and I needed gear to get me through.

'We've got to operate.'

They took me into theatre. A few hours later, after I'd come around from the anaesthetic, the doctor came back to me.

'We had to leave the needle in your arm. It's too close to the tendons and nerves. If we'd damaged them, it could affect how well your hands work. It was too risky. We'll get the infection under control and then you'll have to live with it. But please stop injecting. You'll keep getting infections and even bigger problems. I've got a rehab programme I can get you on.'

But there was only one thing on my mind. As soon as I was discharged, I was out grafting again.

And as the veins all over my body were hardening, I looked for less obvious ones to use – like my legs. I used them but when I needed to give them a rest, because scabs had appeared, I found veins in any other part of my body including my penis, my feet, my arms and even the veins at the side of my eyes. After those injections, I'd wake up with black eyes.

It was all really, really painful. But I didn't care. All that mattered was the high.

So after the doctor had told me, warned me, that I was heading for more and more complications, I still went ahead and kept hitting my body with potentially lethal cocktails of drugs which had a lifetime of physical consequences.

Over the course of the next few months, I injected so often in my legs that they started to get infected. The veins were going rock hard, but I kept on using them.

Sores started to appear and open up. I didn't dress the wounds, so I got more and more infections – made worse because Peter's place had become a full-blown drug den.

It was full of bloody and used needles, blood spots, bloodsoaked clothes, and there were stains all over the sofa, the carpet and bed. The table was just a mess of syringes and sharps boxes, all opened up, their contents scattered on the floor – the potential HIV or hepatitis infection was huge.

It stank of piss and dried blood. Not shit because we never ate and were too constipated from the crack to have a crap.

There were a lot of used mugs on the table, too. Cold tea with mould growing on the top.

If you wanted to show people how low humans could go, Peter's flat would be a good place to start and finish. Disgusting. Filthy. You would not have let a dog go in there.

My 18-year-old self would be totally ashamed.

Every day, when Lal picked me up, we followed the same pattern. By the time he arrived, I was withdrawing from the heroin and chewing my hand off for a hit of crack.

So we went and got £150 worth of gear and brought it back to Peter's so we could shoot up.

Once we'd had a fix, we headed out on the rob for the rest of the day.

I never got nicked the whole time Lal and I went out. We must have done it hundreds of times, but we got away with it every single time.

With the paranoia that crack brings on, I came to think of him as a lucky omen. If he wasn't around, then I would be nervous about grafting.

Our lives were very, very small.

The fence I used was a guy called Mr T. He was good to me to start off with, giving me a third of the value of whatever I nicked.

But then, as I got more and more desperate, he saw that I'd do anything for the cash and reduced it to 25%.

My level of grafting had to go up. I paid Lal £100 for driving, and paid for the petrol. I still needed £500 a day to buy gear, so I'd have to nick £2000-£2500 worth of stuff each and every day just to maintain my habit.

One of my dealers was a guy we called 'Fabulous'. I don't know why; it was just the name he put about. We'd meet him at Seven Kings station, and we'd head down there after seeing Mr T.

My basic order was always £250 worth of crack and £250 worth of heroin (12 white and 12 brown heroin).

White heroin is the purest form of the drug – or it should be, but it's usually cut with baking soda. This is the kind you inject because it needs a higher temperature to burn and smoke it.

Brown heroin isn't as pure or strong because it's not as refined. It's the stuff that's produced in the first stage of production of purification so it's cheaper but is usually smoked because it doesn't dissolve well.

After we met Fabulous, it was straight back to Peter's and we'd spend the night injecting.

By the time I hit 25 years old, the veins in my arms were so hard that I had to boil a kettle and put my hands (wrapped in a towel) in boiling water to get the veins to expand.

Or I'd run a hot bath and sit in it waiting for the veins on my legs to become visible. Then I'd try to inject in the bath.

Sometimes you'd miss the vein altogether and have to keep trying until you hit one. In the end, you'd be sitting in a literal blood bath – just like something out of a horror film.

I had bruises all over me where I'd missed.

After six more months of this, I hadn't got any 'normal' veins left. They were all as hard as concrete and the needles I had just couldn't cope.

So I did something even more stupid.

I started to inject in my groin. This is where the femoral vein is.

To reach the femoral vein, which is buried deep in your groin, you need a two and a half inch needle. When I show that to the kids I give my talks to, there's usually someone who faints. It's a big needle and you have to be really careful.

But the needle isn't the biggest problem. Just next to the femoral vein is the femoral artery which, if you hit it, would cause massive problems.

Sticking a needle in your groin – either side, left or right, I usually alternated if I could remember which I'd injected last – is a messy business.

After about a week, one of my T-shirts was stiff with old blood that I'd mopped up after missing the vein.

What you have to do is check for a pulse on either side of your groin. When you've found it, put the middle finger of your hand over the pulse.

Then you let your index finger rest naturally against the middle finger.

The vein should be at a point just below the upper side of the index finger.

It sounds complicated. And it is. Particularly if you're coming down from a massive high.

Then you have to put the needle into the skin, aiming towards the centre of your body right next to the index finger.

You push the needle in at about 90 degrees to the leg surface – straight, in other words, because you don't want to do it at an angle.

Once it's in a bit, pull back the plunger to make sure the needle is in the vein. (The blood is dark red.)

Then you push the drugs slowly in. Take the needle out slowly. There's almost always some blood that leaks from the puncture hole you make so you should mop that up.

You have to do it quickly because the high from crack hits you like a sledgehammer.

Repeated injections in the femoral vein can cause it to collapse. This usually takes longer in the groin than it does with the veins in the arms because it is a bigger vein, but the consequences are much more serious. The veins in the arms can take a different route using peripheral circulation, but it doesn't work like that in the legs.

The femoral vein is the main route out of the leg. Blocking it means that blood cannot flow through the leg quickly enough to stay healthy and warm. People with collapsing femoral veins often have swollen, painful legs and cold, blue toes. Continuing to inject in the leg can lead to tissue death and amputation of part or all of the leg.

But it's not just repeated injecting in the vein. If you hit the femoral artery, which is just next to it, your risk of lethal complications increases.

Blood in the femoral artery is being pumped down the leg, and injecting into it can cause the blood supply to be blocked causing clots, deep vein thrombosis (DVT), and gangrene in the leg, which can lead to amputation.

DVTs are basically blood clots that form in the deep veins of the leg. They can form near the femoral vein or further down the leg on the calf.

If DVTs form first of all, there is redness, pain and a swelling of the leg. Then you could get chest pains, which tells you the clot may have broken away from the vein and is travelling up through your body and is stuck in the lungs. This is a pulmonary embolism and can kill you.

You know if you've hit the artery because you get bright red, frothy blood rushing down the barrel of the syringe on its own. The pressure from the artery is so high that it can pump hard through the opening you've created with the needle.

As soon as you see that, you've got to stop. Injecting crack into an artery is even more dangerous and, more importantly for an addict, pointless. Arteries take blood away from the heart (veins take it to the heart), so the drugs go straight to your body's tissue, leading to swelling of the skin and unbelievable pain. AND YOU DON'T GET HIGH!

A doctor told me once that even worse than injecting into an artery was injecting into a blood vessel in which you can feel a pulse. It can lead to life-threatening conditions – including arterial bleeding.

If you hit the femoral nerve, you're also in trouble. The nerve controls the muscles that help the knee bend and also supplies feeling to the front of your thigh and the lower part of your leg.

Damaging this nerve can cause walking problems and a loss of feeling in the legs. Not something you want if your only way of getting money for drugs is shoplifting.

What all this means is that I started to do even riskier things to my body. Any infection in that vein or the artery could lead to life-threatening complications that I was in no state to deal with.

And finally, you need to add to this the fact that the lighting at Peter's was low – so I couldn't see what I was doing a lot of the time. Crack addicts don't buy lightbulbs.

I was obsessive, so while Peter and Lal were having two or three hits per night, I was on thirty sometimes fifty a night. My using was far more aggressive than any addict I've ever met.

It was all getting a bit much for Peter, Ian and Lal.

My addiction was through the roof; I had no control at all. I was on Lal's case all the time to go out and rob more, get more drugs and inject more.

If I ran out of crack by 9 o'clock, I wanted more to see me through the night. I knew that Lakeside stayed open till 10.30 p.m., so I'd pester him to take me. He just wanted to have a hit and pass out.

When I didn't go out with Lal, I got nicked quite a lot, so I'd get short prison sentences for shoplifting.

Eventually, Peter had had enough: my using was a problem even for them. It was just too much.

When you use too much, you get a lot of paranoia. I would stand for hours at the spyhole in the front door watching, convinced that someone was coming to get me.

It got so bad one night that I managed to get a hammer and some nails and nailed the door shut.

I think that was the final straw. Peter told me to go.

So I had to find somewhere else.

Over the next few years, all the other addicts in the crack dens were reluctant to let me go into their place to use drugs because my using was too much for them to handle. Even though I was generous because I gave them drugs so I could go to their place, they just couldn't cope with my paranoia and consistent aggressive using. And there was another problem for the addicts – one that no one could have anticipated.

I was generous with my drugs – giving the people who lived in the crack houses gear from my supply to let me stay there for the night. But then over the course of a few weeks, I'd increase their habits. Most users use about £50 worth a day, but with my extra supply they'd move up to £100. When I went to another crack den or got a prison sentence, they realised that they had to up their crime rate to cover their new habit. That was just another reason for other addicts not to hang out with me.

So, I'd find myself using in disabled toilets in KFC and McDonald's till midnight. When I got kicked out of there, I'd go and find somewhere to sleep rough.

CHAPTER TWELVE

I knew Romford. It was where I'd started all my criminal and gang stuff.

But now I'd lost the place that had been my base for a few years.

I headed to Ilford in search of drug dens. They're all over, but I needed somewhere where I could stay longer and I needed a place that was close to shops I could rob.

I got to know two brothers from Glasgow – Russell and Paul. They had a flat. I bought my way in with drugs – giving them hundreds of pounds' worth of crack and heroin. They loved it because they didn't have to do anything to get high.

I was injecting more than ever, but my legs were starting to get really scabby as the injections started to take their toll.

I'd pick at the scabs as well, so they'd get infected. It got bad with my left leg. First, there was a hole that I could put my finger in, then I could put two in and then three.

The smell was also starting to be noticeable.

Lal continued to turn up at my new place every now and again, but I was still out grafting every day.

Robbing, shoplifting, fencing, dealing, injecting. More injecting.

This is my life aged 26. My addiction is out of control.

The constant chance of getting arrested, the extreme risk that every time I injected I might be using an HIV- or hepatitis-infected needle, the possibility of trouble with the dealers or overdosing – none of these bothered me. All I wanted was a syringe-full of heroin and crack, and a sofa to crash out on.

Russell and I were nicked one evening and sent to Pentonville the next day. There was no chance of bail, and I had no money and no drugs. You are put on the bus, taken to jail and processed. We both got three months.

To get admitted, you have to be seen by the prison doctor. If you're a drug addict, you get sent to Rehab Wing, which is the drug-free wing.

Rehab Wing is good because you have a cell to yourself; you're open all day except for maybe lunch and tea. And if you make it outside your cell, you get a job. The trouble was, I was going cold turkey and it was horrendous.

The doctor will give you methadone but only tiny quantities, which get reduced over a five-day period.

So, on day one you'll get 50 mg, 40 on day two, 30 on day three, and so on, until day six you have nothing. 150 mg in total. And there would be some Valium to stop the shaking and to calm you down.

But on the outside, I was doing the equivalent of 150 mg of methadone in one day. So by the end of day one, I was experiencing full cold turkey with not even methadone to help me.

By the end of day two, I was climbing the walls. Desperate for a hit. Hallucinating, vomiting and having constant diarrhoea. I was a shaking, quivering, stinking mess on the cell floor.

These were just the physical symptoms, but enough to make me do anything to take the pain and physical craving away. Your body's withdrawal can last up to 10 days, with days two and three often the lowest point.

But for your mental health, going cold turkey is almost worse. For a start, you can't sleep because your craving is so intense. It's like being shouted at 24/7 by the loudest voice you can imagine. You can't think of anything but getting a hit.

Your whole mind, everything you think of is injecting. Nothing can stop you from thinking, 'I need a fix.'

That time in Pentonville, I didn't sleep for three weeks.

I was just in mental and physical agony in my cell.

Withdrawal has effects that last a long time. I've been through it a dozen times and after each time, I couldn't sleep, my hands shook, I couldn't sit still, I was worried the whole time, paranoid and knackered. And I couldn't find any pleasure in anything. You end up in such a small place – your life, while small when you're on crack, is still smaller when you've been through withdrawal. It takes a long time to be able to open your eyes and see beyond the next minute.

Towards the end of the sentence, I got a job on the hospital servery which was directly beneath Rehab Wing.

When the alarm goes off in prison, all the prisoners are just thrown into the nearest cell, doesn't matter which one, everyone's just chucked in and locked up. This is obviously to stop anyone else getting involved in whatever trouble is kicking off.

But they didn't do that with the guys in the hospital. So if it got nasty in another wing, and prisoners were injured, the screws would bring the prisoners involved into the hospital.

Guys would be coming in wearing spit masks and bent double with blood all over them where they'd self-harmed or stabbed someone. The screws would have given them a dig to make it worse. The prisoners would come through naked or semi-naked, sometimes covered in their own shit.

The screws would hold them down, pin them to the ground, face down, and one of the male nurses would come along with a large syringe.

It was called a 'liquid cosh', which was a mixture of amitriptyline and Largactil. It's also been called 'coma in a bottle'. Largactil was used on prisoners during the Strangeways riots in 1990. It's heavy-duty stuff. Knocks anyone out.

They'd inject them with this huge needle and chuck them in the padded cell. You'd hear the door being kicked and punched for about 10 minutes and then it would all go quiet.

Working on the hospital hotplate, I had to provide these guys in the padded cell their food. I'd leave it outside the door, and the guards would have to take it in.

After three or four days in the cell, they'd be let out. Jesus, that was a horrendous sight. They'd shuffle out, heads down, dribbling, hair matted with blood and shit, eyes shot to hell. They were like shells of people.

You'd see a lot of that in the hospital. Big, big men, 6 feet 5, 20 stone, just shuffling, totally coshed. Out of it. Sedated. More often than not, they had massive mental health problems – arms full of scars from self-harm. I wondered sometimes how they were still alive, as the injuries they caused themselves looked so severe.

Anyway, that was where I saw horrendous mental health problems. And I thought that they needed to be in a psychiatric hospital not a prison, but that wasn't going to happen. They were kept there heavily sedated all the time. Horrendous.

I was released after six weeks – half of my three-month sentence. I was just coming out of the cold turkey and the physical effects of withdrawal at least were calming down.

When you get released from prison, you get an envelope with a single cash payment of £60 (as it was back then) called a discharge grant to help you get home and buy a few necessities.

Russell and I were released at the same time. I had been clean for near enough six weeks, but even after going through the living hell of cold turkey locked up in a prison cell, I had only two words in my head: Crack. Heroin.

We went back to Ilford, scored some gear – crack, heroin and Valium – and a couple of cans of Kestrel Super.

I cooked up the gear, took the Valium and drank the lager.

Bang.

Overdose.

The next thing I knew, I opened my eyes to see paramedics leaning over me, my jeans ripped apart where they'd been trying to find a vein to insert an IV.

I knew nothing about what had happened.

For addicts who've just been through cold turkey, it's common to have an overdose if you go straight back to what you were used to taking before.

The body just can't cope with the 'normal' dose you were used to before you got clean.

My heart had stopped and the paramedics had defibbed me – I'd been dead for I don't know how long.

For once, I hadn't gone straight to a public toilet to shoot up. I don't know whether it was because I had been six weeks clean and wanted to enjoy the hit more, but Russell and I had gone back to his to inject.

As soon as he saw what was happening to me, he called the ambulance. Saved my life. If I'd gone to a public toilet, I'd be dead.

They blue-lighted me to hospital and rushed me into A&E hooked up to an IV. The doctors were coming in and out doing blood tests, checking my vital signs and being very concerned.

But I was getting bored. I was sitting in A&E wearing a hospital gown with nothing to do except be looked at, prodded and assessed by the doctors.

'Right, I'm going,' I said to a doctor who'd just pulled back the curtain and come in.

'But we've got your treatment lined up.'

'No, not doing that.'

But I had no clothes because the paramedics had ripped my jeans. So I got some blue scrubs and walked out of the hospital. Straight to Russell's place.

'What the hell are you doing?'

'I want some gear, so I'm going out grafting. Want to come?'

And that was it. Within a few hours of overdosing and my heart stopping for I don't know how long, I was out shoplifting to score more gear.

Later that afternoon, I was injecting.

That was the extent of the illness of addiction.

At Russell and Paul's, I was with two people who wanted exactly the same as me. That meant, though, that I was injecting more and more and more.

The clots in my legs were getting worse. The wounds and sores just weren't healing. I could see the bone because the flesh has just pulled away.

I didn't want to waste money on bandages and plasters.

So I got a packet of nappies and wrapped one around my left leg.

But that didn't hide the smell.

One morning, Russell said to me, 'Paul, your legs are rotten. They stink.'

I thought I'd better to go to hospital to get them sorted. So I hobbled along to Oldchurch Hospital in Romford.

The doctors warned me that I'd lose my leg unless I let them treat it.

When they admitted me, they gave me 100 mg of methadone a day to help with the withdrawal. It made me laugh.

That amount would kill a lot of people, but my tolerance was so high that it hardly touched the sides.

They gave me Valium, too, to help manage the withdrawal. But they wouldn't give me anything to help with the crack withdrawal, so I was missing that huge crack high.

Oldchurch Hospital was an old-fashioned Victorian building. It was built as a workhouse and changed to a hospital in the 1950s.

It was quite a big place and very busy. There were over 500 patients, not counting the people who attended as outpatients, so the nurses and doctors always had lots to do.

The wards were the kind that had 30 to 40 beds on them. I was just one of many patients they had to look after, so I very quickly saw that there was a chance to do my own bit of medication.

Just over the road from the hospital, there was a shopping centre called The Brewery.

The first day I watched the nurses and doctors carefully. In prison, you get used to watching the screws' shift patterns; so you get to know when's a good time to do something that you don't want them to see.

I used the same idea to work out when the doctors and nurses wouldn't be paying attention to me.

There was a handover every day at 3 o'clock. The shift changed and the nurses all went into a room at the end of the ward to be briefed by the sister or senior nurse about all us patients.

There was usually one nurse left on the ward, but she was rushed off her feet because she had 40 patients to keep an eye on.

Technically, I wasn't allowed off the ward, but who was going to notice?

The meeting took about 40 minutes.

The second day I was there, I got myself ready before the handover by putting my clothes on under the hospital gown.

As soon as the nurses had disappeared into the meeting room, I took off the gown, put my trainers on and hobbled out of the ward. Just as I did when I was shoplifting.

If you walk with enough confidence, people rarely give you a second look.

So I had a window of about 40 minutes.

I raced over to The Brewery, which took five minutes. It had JD Sports, TK Maxx and a few designer shops. I grabbed as much as I could. I was so experienced that I could pick up about £1500 worth of stuff in a single visit. It was very, very easy.

I hobbled back to the hospital and hid my haul in the bushes on the hospital grounds.

Then I walked back onto the ward as if nothing had happened. The nurse didn't bat an eyelid, and I got back into my gown.

Hospitals are fantastic places to get away with stuff. After 20 minutes I asked to go out for a smoke (I didn't smoke) and rang Mr T from the public payphone.

I arranged to meet him later to fence the stuff I'd nicked. When the time came, I just went for another cigarette and we did the deal in the car park. Now I had a pocket full of cash.

On the way back in, I phoned my dealer and arranged to meet him in the car park within an hour.

It was that easy.

In the meantime, I was getting friendly with a lot of the patients' families on the ward. They wanted to know everything about me: my leg, my drug addiction, my crimes and my life. I still had the cheeky boy air about me and I was naturally chatty.

When they found out about the shoplifting, I asked them if they wanted anything from the shops – sportswear, aftershave, perfume, that kind of thing.

Quickly, I was nicking stuff to order for the families of the other patients. My service was better than Amazon as far as these people were concerned.

I made more money because I didn't have to fence the goods to Mr T and I could just call the dealer straight away.

These law-abiding, completely normal, everyday people's families were happy to buy this stuff from me, knowing full well it was stolen, knowing full well I was a drug addict and knowing full well that I'd be giving the money to a drug dealer.

They were playing a small part in my illness by enabling me, which shows that normal people, too, can be just as selfish and greedy as so-called criminals.

I was in the hospital for nearly three months and still managed to take crack and heroin while I was there – morning, noon and night.

And I kept taking the methadone, so my habit was getting even bigger. But to inject, I still needed teaspoons, tablespoons and needles.

There were lots of spoons on the tea trolley. So I'd go into the ward kitchen and help myself to the spoons. When you burn the crack and heroin, the bottom of the spoon goes black. I couldn't really put the spoons back into circulation once I'd smoked from them, so I threw them in the bin.

After a few weeks, I heard the two old tea ladies moaning that all the spoons had gone missing. The kitchen staff were all scratching their heads wondering where all the spoons had gone.

I'd got through hundreds of spoons and ended up nicking loads from the hospital canteen.

The needles I had to steal from the bandage room. I could reuse them, so didn't need that many.

And then to actually inject, I went for a shower.

Between 30 to 40 times a day.

'You're having a lot of showers,' the nurses said.

'Yeah, need to keep myself clean, don't I?'

Again, because it was so busy all the time, it worked to my advantage.

Visiting time was 5 p.m. I'd sell the gear I'd just nicked and go out to meet the dealer.

One evening, I noticed they had a DD box (dangerous drugs) in one of the rooms on the ward near the office. At 9 p.m. there was another handover and two auxiliary nurses came on (who did bed changes and stuff like that) with one trained nurse who gave out medication.

I noticed when I walked past the room where the DD box was that the trained nurse would be in there allocating all the DD for people on the ward. I thought to myself, 'Whatever's in that box is going to get me out of my nut.'

But how could I get in there when it was locked unless someone was actually dispensing the drugs?

Back then, before mobiles were everywhere, there used to be a public telephone on wheels that patients could use. 10p or 20p.

So I waited for her to open up the cabinet in the DD room. The auxiliary nurses would be busy looking after someone, changing sheets or a bag or something – remember, there were 40 sick people on the ward. Then I'd call the office number from the telephone on wheels. It would ring and ring. Eventually, she'd get fed up and go into the office which was about a 30-yard walk from the drug treatment room, so I had a 30-second window to get in, grab as much as I could out of the box and get back to my bed before being caught.

My haul would be a combination of morphine, Valium, tramadol and sleeping tablet suppositories. An hour later in the toilet, I was swallowing Valium, shoving sleeping tablets up my arse and injecting crack.

A few times they'd find me passed out, obliterated, smashed off my nut on the bathroom floor.

I was using the hospital as a drug den.

Joanne tracked me down and started to come and visit with her mum.

She was worried about me and wanted me to come back and live with them, but only if I got clean.

I said, 'I can't come off the methadone.'

'OK, but get rid of the crack and heroin.'

I said I'd think about it, and then carried on.

The doctors were getting concerned that my legs weren't healing. They couldn't work out why the wounds were still there and new ones were forming. They had no idea I was sneaking out of the hospital every day. They were baffled because they were pumping me full of antibiotics but those drugs weren't having any effect.

The blood results would come back, but they couldn't work out what was wrong.

So they decided to do a skin graft to see if they could move the process on a bit faster.

I thought it'd take a while for them to get around to it, but they appeared one afternoon just as I'd got back from having a hit in the shower.

I was off my nut.

'We're taking you down to theatre in an hour. Can you put on your hospital gown?'

They took me down, but instead of giving me a general anaesthetic, they decided to give me an epidural, which numbs you from the waist down. I was sitting there completely cracked out of my head for three hours while they operated.

The doctors decided that for the next three days they'd keep me on an epidural anaesthetic because they needed the time to allow the skin graft to take.

They put a line into my spine and a doctor came around to feed in the anaesthetic. 'Don't touch the line. If it comes out, you could be paralysed.'

So, I wasn't allowed to move for three days, which was a problem because I couldn't go shoplifting.

I deliberately ripped the tube out of my spine so the numbness would wear off and I could go grafting. Blood was pumping out of my back. A nurse rushed over, her face drained in shock.

'Paul, how did that happen? Jesus, you could have permanently damaged your spinal cord. Paralysed for life.'

'It just came out in my sleep.'

She didn't believe me, but I didn't care. I just needed a fix.

Then one afternoon, as I got back from a shopping trip, I literally bumped into one of the nurses. She was leaving early and I nearly knocked her over as I ran back into the hospital thinking I was late.

She noticed the bags. The next day, she had a look through the locker drawers when I was having a shower and found my stash and some of the dangerous drugs from the cabinet.

This nurse put it all together – quite smart really – and told the ward sister.

The sister asked me into the office just before handover and confronted me with all the evidence.

'Come on, Paul. That's not on. We're trying to save your leg. Use this as an opportunity to get clean – take the methadone and stop the other stuff. You can do it.'

She was giving me a chance. If I hadn't been so off my head all the time, I might have listened to her.

As it was, I went out the next afternoon and was caught coming back in again.

They chucked me out of the hospital for abusing the system.

I'd been there nearly three months and, if I'm honest, I was comfortable there: I managed to take even more drugs and made a ton of money.

My legs were still getting worse because my habit had increased, and I'm sure all these law-abiding citizens who were happy to get knock-off goods and feed my addiction were gutted when I got chucked out.

I got my methadone prescription and moved back in with Joanne.

For a while, I tried to keep straight. I didn't go out shoplifting and stuck to the methadone.

I got back to the house one day after I'd picked up my prescription.

As I was about to put my key in the door, Kay opened it.

She had a face like thunder.

'Get in this house.'

'What have I done now?'

'Joanne's pregnant. You've got to sort yourself, get a job, get off that methadone.'

'OK, I'll do it. I promise.'

CHAPTER THIRTEEN

It took three months.

I moved in and got off the gear. I tried to play the dad-to-be role and things for a while looked as though they were going to work out.

Then one day, I was out, bumped into Russell and that was it.

Relapsed.

Joanne rang me.

'What's happened? Where are you?'

'I'm back on the gear.'

'What do you mean? What about the baby?'

'I don't know. Have an abortion.'

'I don't want to get rid of it. Please come back to me.'

I put the phone down and blocked her.

Back on the routine: grafting, fencing, injecting.

But I wasn't as quick or as mobile as I was, so I got nicked again for shoplifting.

I was sent back to Pentonville for four months.

Cold turkey hit again, but I got through it OK.

It was back to the old prison routine: Slop out, breakfast, work, lunch, slop out, work, dinner, association, bed.

One afternoon after lunch, I was lying on my bed in the cell. I had about three weeks left of my sentence and I was already thinking about life when I got out. Back then, I was still asleep, I had no thought beyond going and doing the same thing all over.

I had an illness: I was a drug addict, so that's what I did. And what else was I going to do? I couldn't get a job; I didn't have qualifications. Besides, I didn't want one.

There wasn't any alternative for me. I was unconscious, asleep, going through my life without any awareness of what I was doing – the harm I was doing to myself and everyone around me. I didn't have a defence against relapsing because addiction drives everything you do. It's an illness that controls you totally.

A letter appeared under the cell door. In those days, the screws would deliver the handwritten letters – after they'd been checked – but I'd never had one before and wasn't expecting anything.

My cellmate picked it up, looked at the envelope and tossed it at me.

'For you.'

My name was written on the envelope.

I never got letters or visitors. I was alone.

I recognised the handwriting.

It was Joanne's.

I opened the envelope and read what she'd written to me.

> *Dear Paul*
>
> *I know you're in Pentonville. Please let me come and see you. I'm still pregnant and give birth in two weeks. I can come and see you.*
>
> *Love*
>
> *Joanne*

She'd called all the hospitals and prisons. She'd found out that I'd been sent down and tracked me down to Pentonville.

She phoned up to book a visit. Two days later, the guard came to collect me from my cell and took me to the visitor centre. I'd never been there before. It was August 1995 and a really hot day.

The visitor centre at that point was a large room similar to a school assembly hall. The tables were laid out like when kids are doing GCSEs or A-levels – all in rows, one in front of the other. Some tables had just one chair opposite the prisoner while others had two or three.

The prisoners grabbed as many chairs as they needed.

I guess there were about 80 tables in total.

I was at the back of the hall facing the door. It must have been 120 yards long.

My legs were jiggling up and down. I was excited.

By now, I'd been clean for a while. After the five days of methadone I'd gone through, I hadn't had anything more (I was on Rehab Wing again so it was drug-free).

I was eating as well – prison food, but food, so I was gaining a bit of weight. I'd been working in the kitchen so could always help myself to a bit of extra.

The door opened and she was the first to come in.

The picture in my mind of her walking through that door is one I'll never forget. It'll never fade. She was dressed all in white – white dungarees, white sandals and a white T-shirt, gold necklace, big blue eyes and blonde curly hair looking absolutely beautiful. Stunning. She was a healthy glowing picture of a pregnant woman.

Everyone was looking at her as she walked slowly through the room. It was as though she was lit up. I sat there amazed. An angel.

Her eyes were searching me out. When she spotted me, she gave me a wave and carried on her waddle past the other prisoners.

As she made her way past the tables, the room got quieter and quieter.

I could tell what a lot of the other prisoners were thinking.

She really looked beautiful.

I swelled up with pride.

She'd managed to get here from Romford while eight and a half months pregnant. It was a hot day, so the trains and tubes must have been a sweaty nightmare.

Joanne sat down – exhausted from the effort of travelling in the heat.

The guards got her some water. She was two weeks from giving birth.

We had an hour.

In that hour, she cried her eyes out and literally begged me that when I got out of prison – which was in a week's time – to promise her that I'd move in with her (she had her own flat at this point).

'Please, Paul, I've moved out of Mum's house. Got my own place. A flat.'

I nodded.

'But I've got no money coming in. I left my job. Please come back and get a job. We're going to have a little baby. She'll need looking after.'

It was the first time I'd heard that I was going to be a dad to a little girl.

For the second time, I was blown away.

The reality of being a dad started to work on me. I could picture taking her to the park, playing on the swings, building her a little doll's house or magic cottage in the garden.

I had all those pictures in my head in a few seconds.

I nodded again.

'So will you come back and get a job?'

'Yeah. I'll go back to scaffolding.'

'And you'll never touch drugs again?'

'Never. I'm clean now. Off the methadone. I'm not taking crack or heroin. I'm the cleanest I've been in years. Not on anything.'

'Promise?'

She cried.

'I promise.'

I looked at her – tears falling down her face from her red and swollen eyes.

After a minute, I said, 'Look, when the baby's born, when I've got the job and we're a bit sorted, will you marry me?'

She held my gaze and swallowed. Wiping the tears away, she smiled and said, 'Yeah, I will.'

We both got very emotional at this point. It felt like we'd been on such a long journey together and it had been really hard, really traumatic, but now, at last, perhaps we were getting to the happy conclusion.

The guard came round and said, 'OK, wrap your visit up.'

I gave her a massive hug and a kiss and said, 'Look, I'll see you again next week.'

The guard led her out of one door. As she left, she turned and gave me a huge smile and a wave. I was taken out of the door at the opposite end by a guard who knew me well because I'd been in so often.

'Is that your girlfriend?'

'Yeah.' I grinned.

'You're a lucky man.'

'Yeah. We're going to have a baby, get married. I've had enough now. I'm done.'

'Well, if you don't get out of prison and sort your life out for her, you're crazy.'

And I knew he was right.

I left that visiting room on cloud nine. I don't think there was a happier, prouder person in the prison that day. Maybe not in London, either.

Going back to my cell, I just beamed all the way. And as I walked in and threw myself on the bed, I told my cellmate that things were now working out. That I was sorted and had never been happier.

My cellmate was a mad character called Noel. The whole prison loved him – he was wild but funny and good with it.

I sat with Noel and told him about the visit:

'Just had the best visit, having a baby, getting married, getting out next week, and then I've had enough, I'm done. Going to make a real life now.'

'Fair play to you.'

And then I told him all about it again. And again.

Unfortunately, Noel was released three days after that visit, and the guard came to my cell the following evening and gave me the news that Noel had relapsed the day he got out of prison. They'd found him dead in a public toilet. Heroin overdose.

That week dragged on and on. I phoned Joanne a couple of times.

We were on the phone for as long as we were allowed, had great conversations, made loads of plans and both really excited about the future.

I really couldn't have been happier, and I don't think I'd been as happy as this since we moved into the pub.

And that was a different kind of happy – this was all about what my life was going to be. Back then, it was just about the present and the freedom of roaming through the big pub.

Now I really could see an amazing time ahead. With Joanne. And my little baby girl.

The night before I was released, I rang her and said I'd go round to the flat, drop my clothes off and go and see if I could get my old scaffolding job back.

'Are you excited?'

'Yeah, I'm really excited.'

'Me, too. Can't wait.'

'I'll cook you your favourite – mash and tuna.'

That was the first ever meal she had cooked for me.

'I don't care what I have, I'll just be so happy to see you. I'll tell you what, though, why don't we go out for pie and mash at that place in Romford?'

'Where we had our first date?'

'Yeah.'

'I'd love that. I was so nervous that day.'

'Yeah, me too. Great. We'll do that, then. See you tomorrow. I love you.'

I don't think I slept that night. I kept saying to myself that it was my last night in prison and picturing my life ahead.

The following morning I was taken down to reception.

When they release you from prison, they give you back the clothes you were arrested in and the belongings they took off you when you started your sentence, which wasn't much.

And they give you a little brown envelope with £60 in cash, the discharge grant, and a travel warrant, which is a single ticket to wherever you've said you're going to be staying when you're released. In my case, that was Romford.

So I got my travel warrant and thought, 'Right, I'll get the train to Romford, go round to her place, have a decent bit of grub with her and give her the £60 for food and baby stuff – milk and nappies – because she's had very little at this point.' It was down to me to be responsible for her and the baby.

Then I'll go and see Tony and try to get a job. It'll be the start of my new life.

Simple really.

As I was waiting to be released, I walked into reception with six other prisoners. They were all being let out as well.

I knew one of them. I'd used with him before. Another addict.

We waited in a room for about an hour. Prison's a lot about waiting around.

I got chatting to the guy who said, 'I'm going to meet a dealer in a minute.'

And I said, 'I'm not doing it. I've had enough. I'm done. Going to see my girlfriend. Have tuna and mash.'

We got released. I walked off with him.

He went straight to an off-licence.

He went in and got a beer. I thought, 'I'll just get a tin of beer as well. Just to celebrate my release.'

I got a beer. Drank it. Got another one. Drank it. The first tin of lager poisoned my whole thinking, and the craving for crack and heroin was overwhelming. It was just too powerful to resist. The illness took control of me.

An hour later, I was in a crack den using the last of the discharge grant injecting heroin and crack into my groin.

Within three hours, I was back down the West End shoplifting.

I never went to Joanne's. I totally destroyed all her hopes and dreams of me being a decent father, of getting married and creating a happy family. I was yanked back into that dark place unable to resist the power of the addiction.

We didn't get married. I wasn't there for the birth of my daughter. I didn't get a job.

I didn't see my daughter for 14 years. To be honest, I didn't care about her first birthday, her first Christmas, her first steps, her calling me Dad. Joanne having to bring up my daughter as a single mother didn't even cross my mind.

The illness of addiction had made me so selfish that no one else mattered. Just me and drugs. They were the only things that counted.

Not for one minute did I know or care that I was a dad.

CHAPTER FOURTEEN

This beautiful woman, Joanne, who I was in love with offered me a second and a third chance. I turned my back on it because of my illness.

I had this beautiful chance of setting up a life with this fantastic woman and my daughter. And I totally disregarded it.

Instead, the illness made me choose to live a stinking, thieving, lonely existence, hobbling through life with the threat of getting HIV or hepatitis, or of dying of an overdose. I had no comforts, no food, no entertainment, no friends. I never celebrated Christmas or my birthday.

Worst of all was that I had no dreams, no desires and no passions. I didn't want to do anything apart from go out every day, get as much money as possible and spend every single penny on drugs. There was no ambition or ideas about what to do or focusing on what you're good at. You're just fixated on the next hit – trying to score as much as possible.

Every day is an absolute nightmare. You wake up terrified that you won't get the money for a hit. You rob and graft to get it, knowing you could be nicked at any moment, and then you spend agonising amounts of time hanging around waiting for the drug dealer to turn up whenever it suits them. You use, and then you're back on the same cycle. There was no rest or let-up.

You are a slave to heroin and crack. You do whatever they want you to do.

And I gave up that beautiful future with Joanne to do all this shit again.

I moved back to Harold Hill with Peter and Ian. Back to the place where I'd tried to nail the door shut when I was paranoid. Back to the place of Hell.

There was a guy I knew from my schooldays called Gary. He had a car. So I latched onto him like I did Lal – anyone with a car basically, as it saved me getting taxis everywhere and it saved me having to walk because my legs were still really bad.

Gary liked a bit of crack. He worked as well, but other times he'd take me out shoplifting.

So, I was back at square one. I was injecting hundreds of pounds of crack and heroin every day, going out shoplifting to pay for my habit and living in absolute squalor.

One day, I went back up to Ilford to do some shoplifting and score some gear. I ended up in a crack den up there.

Russell and his brother walked in. It had been a while since I'd seen them – since he saved my life after I overdosed.

Russell got a bit leery with me that night. He was a bit cheeky, and I was off my head.

We started to exchange words and he riled me. I knocked him out with one punch. Just one of those moments where I went a bit mad and I wanted him to shut up. So I decked him and walked out, which wasn't a wise move, as Russell was renowned for carrying a knife and using it. He'd cut and hurt a lot of people in Ilford over the previous few years.

A month later, I was in another crack den up that way. I left to go back to another place I knew in Romford, and as I walked down the street, in the distance under the street lamps, I saw three figures coming towards me. I realised it was Russell, his brother Paul and a Scouse bloke.

Russell and his brother recognised me, and I saw their hands go into their pockets. The brothers pulled out butcher's knives, and the Scouser reached into his coat and weighed a hammer in his hand.

They came walking towards me screaming, shouting, swearing. I couldn't hear the words as I was focusing on Russell's blade.

I tried to grab the knife with my right hand. He pulled it back and as he did, it sliced the palm of my hand open. There was a massive gash with warm blood pumping out.

Then he tried to slash my face. Automatically, I put my left hand up to protect myself. The knife nearly cut my left middle finger deeply.

As I was doing that, I felt this sharp pain twice in my back side. I looked around and saw that Paul, his brother, had stabbed me.

The Scouser hit me on the back of the head with the hammer. He just grazed me but still did a lot of damage. After about 30 seconds, they had done their job and run off.

I had blood pouring out of my hand, my arse. I was losing a lot of blood and concussed from the hammer. I collapsed on the street.

A black cab driver stopped, bundled me into his cab and rushed me to hospital.

When I got to A&E, they gave me a blood transfusion and sewed up my arse and hand. I'd lost a lot of blood, but the doctors had saved my life. Again.

And a cabbie had saved me, too. If it hadn't been for him – and the fact that he was kind enough to stop and help someone he didn't know from Adam – I'd be dead.

When I left hospital, my hands were in bandages to protect the stitches from getting infected. But the moment I turned up at Peter's, it was inevitable that I would come into contact with something dirty.

Sure enough, my hands swelled up within a couple of days of getting back. They'd got infected.

So I was walking around with my hands all blown up and the stitches still in. I couldn't even wipe my own arse let alone cook up and inject.

I had to ask anyone else around to prepare the gear and inject me.

And this meant that I was sharing even more needles. Breaking open the sharps box, pulling out whichever was least bloody, rinsing it out and then reusing. Over the course of the 15 plus years I was doing this, I must have shared needles well over 1000 times.

Unbelievably, I never got HIV or hepatitis. I've been tested nine times. Each time I was absolutely terrified because I was convinced that I'd be unlucky and it would be positive.

Every time the result came back from the nurse it was negative, and each time it made me realise how fortunate I was.

The risk of infection in a drug den is so high that it's a miracle I didn't catch something lethal while I lived there. Particularly if you take into account the number of shared needles I used.

Getting beaten up by Russell and the other two just meant that I avoided Ilford if I could.

I gave a talk in 2020 at Nottingham Medical School and mentioned this one thing to a medic there. He looked at me as though I was a ghost. He thought I should have died.

It was a story that I had only just remembered, and it scares me a bit now when I think of it. And the physical scars that I see daily scare me too.

Around this time, I bumped into another addict on my journey through the crack dens. He used to get a monthly script for temazepam and Valium. About 100 of each tablet from a private doctor.

When you take temazepam on top of heroin, it actually makes it stronger, more powerful. And if you add alcohol, then it's stronger still.

That was exactly the kind of thing I loved. When I wasn't getting the same high as I used to, here was something that took it up a level.

One night I got back to this one crack den where I spent a lot of time. I'd been thieving so was sorted for drugs and had a load of Kestrel Super with me. I swapped some crack for some downers (Valium), ate about 20 blue Valium (200 mg in total – a lot), necked the Kestrels, had a hit of crack, had a hit of heroin and the next thing I know I'm passed out on the sofa. Then I woke up.

As I opened my eyes, by my feet was a massive pile of leather jackets. There were seven.

I looked a bit closer and saw that they were Hugo Boss with £700 price tags.

'Whose are those jackets?'

'They're yours.'

'What do you mean they're mine?'

'You went out an hour ago in a cab to Lakeside.'

All the jackets had alarms on them. I realised that I must have got up, booked a taxi, got to Lakeside just before it closed and nicked £4900 worth of leather jackets.

I don't remember doing it.

The whole thing must have taken an hour yet I had no memory whatsoever.

That's what temazepam does to you. It gives you total blackouts.

I got on the phone to fence and had a bonus that night: an extra pocketful of crack and heroin. And there I was injecting crack and heroin in my groin for the rest of the night.

By now I was 27 and the familiar routine life was back in full swing. I moved from crack den to crack den. Sometimes 10 in 10 nights in 10 different towns and cities – anywhere from my normal haunts in Essex to outer London boroughs, to places in Hertfordshire. I can't emphasise enough that they are everywhere. Drug addiction has infected every single place in this country. Rich or poor – it doesn't matter.

I kept the same clothes on and used whatever T-shirt or piece of material I could find at the drug den to mop up the blood that spurted from my groin after each injection.

Inject, rob, fence, inject, inject, sleep, rob, fence…it went round and round 24/7.

I described a day in the life of a crack and heroin addict at the start of the book, and it was this time of my life that I was really talking about.

Because the days were pretty much all the same and I was off my nut for all of them, the images I have are blurred.

But like I said at the opening, a crack den is a crack den. You might get a different bit of furniture, a radio or an armchair, but most of them are stripped back to the basics.

They stink, they're dark, they're lonely, but for me and many others we called them home maybe just for a few hours because there was nowhere else for us to go.

Each time a needle went into my groin, I knew I was slowly dying – physically and spiritually. My left leg was now so bad I could see the bone. The wound was so big I could put my fist into it. And it absolutely stank.

I had to dress my legs every day in nappies.

When I got out of hospital the last time – after the skin graft – I used bandages for a while when I was at Joanne's. But as soon as I relapsed and got out of jail that last time, I couldn't be bothered to get proper dressings for the legs.

So I decided the next best thing – absorbent and cheap – would be nappies.

I nicked a few packets from a supermarket and started to use them every day.

The thing is that the wounds were sticky, so pulling the nappy off was excruciating.

It would take half an hour to ease it off. Every morning I sat in the bath full of cold water to loosen the nappy – and as I peeled another section back, an inch or two of rotten, dark skin would come off with it. The water was cold because the crack den never had a boiler.

By the end of it, the bath was full of blood and skin. It was disgusting. The skin graft I had in hospital was long gone.

While the wound on my left leg was gaping, my right leg got infected. It swelled up like a balloon and went jet black. This was from the blood clots in my leg that were stopping the flow of blood from the top of the leg.

Even getting to the bath in the morning was a trial. It took me 10 minutes to manoeuvre my legs from the disgusting sofa I'd slept on so I could put my feet on the needle-strewn floor. The pain of the blood trying to rush to my feet was agony. There were bloodstained T-shirts, pants and socks all over the place as I hobbled to the bathroom.

Every time I had to change the nappy, it took half an hour and it was excruciatingly painful. And the smell made other addicts gag. It was horrendous.

Even the other crackheads would complain about the smell.

My legs were rotting. I was in real danger.

But I didn't care because my mind was set and focused on my next fix.

When I was 28, I bumped into a guy called Big Steve. We remembered each other from our schooldays and realised that we used to hang around with each other as kids. He was big into bodybuilding as well, so a useful lump to have around if there was any trouble.

He had become addicted to crack but was a car salesman during the day.

Steve had a brand-new car as part of his job. I latched onto him like I had the others.

So for a couple of years he would take me to Lakeside or Bluewater or Chelmsford to go shoplifting after work. It was busy at 5 p.m., so I didn't get nicked often. We'd go most days including weekends.

Each time I thought I was running out of options for transport or a place to inject and sleep, something new would come up.

I developed this ability, even when I was off my head in some drug den or other, that if someone came in – it didn't matter if I knew them or not – and they put their car keys down anywhere – a kitchen counter, a coffee table or even a chair – I'd be up, alert and over to them in seconds flat.

It's as if the sound was a trigger for me, and I started to charm the driver into taking me to a shopping centre to go grafting.

There was one time when it all worked perfectly. The driver came in just after 9 o'clock at night. I'd had a hit but heard the jangle of keys. I walked over and started on my chat.

By 9.10 p.m. we were racing around the M25 to Lakeside. We parked up at 9.30, and basically I had half an hour to rob as much as I could. I walked to a department store thinking it was the easiest place to get what I needed. The good thing was that the cleaners were already in, hoovering away, there were almost no customers and the salespeople were cashing up, so their attention was diverted away from me.

The problem was a big one. The security guard had already locked up most of the doors and was standing by the only open one. He had his keys in one hand and a radio in the other. There was no way I could sneak past him with a load of stuff.

I walked in and piled up the gear I wanted to take, then I went over to the security guy and tapped him on the shoulder. I spoke to him as though I was his best friend.

'Here, mate, there's a couple of guys at the back of the store nicking loads of perfume and aftershave.'

His eyes lit up – here's an easy collar he probably thought. 'Yeah? What do they look like?'

I gave him some random description, watched him puff out his chest and then race off after non-existent criminals. Just 10 seconds later, I was also marching off but in the opposite direction, out of the door with £2000 worth of goods. I just picked up my haul and walked out.

My genius head – my illness, actually – came up with this plan; I used it a few times over the years.

When I hit 30, nine years after I'd started using heroin, my life was becoming really painful.

I'd probably spent 18 months in prison in total and I'd tried a few times to get clean. Nothing apart from the routine of injecting and grafting seemed to work for me.

I'd go into prison, maybe get clean for a month or three but start again as soon as I was out. But prison, even if it didn't rehabilitate me, gave my body some respite. At least for those few weeks I'd be clean and my body was grateful for the rest.

One night in a crack den, I met a guy called Mark. He was staying in another crack den that was owned by someone called Frank. Frank didn't use at all and spent his time at his girlfriend's, so he let Mark stay there.

As far as crack dens go, it was good – it had heating for a start, and a TV. Mark smoked a bit of heroin but didn't inject. We got on all right, and having hot water made a massive difference to taking off the nappies.

I didn't have any stuff to move, so I just turned up and started to inject and kipped on the couch. And went out shoplifting every day.

One night, about a week after I'd moved in, he said to me, 'Inject me. I just want to see what it's like.'

I said, 'Don't bother, no way, you won't be able to stop once you start.'

But he kept on and on at me until eventually I agreed. So I got a small syringe about an inch long and put £5 worth of heroin in it.

He sat back on the sofa and put his arm out. I easily found the vein and injected him. Within a minute, his eyes had glazed over and he fell back into the sofa to enjoy the buzz.

I went to cook up my stuff in the kitchen. As I was doing this, I tried to have a conversation with him, but I wasn't getting any replies.

I thought, 'He's quiet.'

After about five minutes, I went back into the living room and he was just lying, bent over, head on the floor, the rest of his body on the sofa.

He was dead.

I panicked. Felt for a pulse in his neck. There was nothing. His lips were blue and his face was grey.

I didn't know how to do CPR, so I got him on his back, screamed his name, slapped his face and chucked cold water over him. Nothing. No response.

My last option was mouth-to-mouth. After about five minutes, there was still nothing.

I was four storeys up in a block of flats. There was no mobile phone – if you had one, you usually had to sell it at some point when you didn't have cash – and I didn't even know the address of the apartment. I hadn't been there long enough to take notice of that kind of thing.

That meant I couldn't ring an ambulance because I didn't know where we were.

So I kept trying to revive him. He just lay there in front of me. Not breathing.

My mind was blank. I couldn't think what to do.

I went out into the hallway knowing that I needed to leave this crack den, because eventually he would be found and I'd be questioned about what had happened.

I made my way to the front door to leave, grabbing any evidence of me being there. I got to the street door and heard a cough. I thought I was hearing things, but it happened again.

I ran back into the living room and noticed that Mark had sick coming from his mouth. And he was moving and breathing. The relief was overwhelming.

I picked him up and walked down the stairs with him in a fireman's lift.

It was raining outside.

I got him out into the fresh air and turned his face so the rain fell on it.

Somehow, I knew I had to keep him awake; he could die if he went back to sleep.

By the end of two hours we were soaking, but he was more conscious. He had no idea what had happened to him.

I kept watch on him overnight. He had a black eye and one of his teeth was knocked out because I'd been hitting him so hard the night before.

Rather that than have him die.

He didn't inject again.

After about a week, I moved on to another crack den. I didn't see him for years, but then many years later when I was clean and sober, I went back to Essex.

I was in Tesco's in Collier Row buying a sandwich. This guy came up and tapped me on the shoulder.

'All right, Paul Hannaford. You look like you're doing really well. I've heard about the school stuff you've been doing.'

I looked at this guy. He looked unwell – yellow, skinny, jaundiced. I had no idea who he was. I think he could see that I didn't recognise him.

'It's Mark,' he said.

He told me that he'd quit drugs but had become an alcoholic. I looked in his basket and there was a litre and a half bottle of Smirnoff.

And I had complete empathy for him because I knew how much pain he was in.

Every time I see someone like that from my past, it makes me more determined to keep telling the kids how to avoid doing the stuff I did and getting to the point where your life is controlled by one thing.

It's so sad to see what happened to all these guys.

It was a miracle that I got clean and sober.

But that was far into the future.

I didn't think I could go much further down the spiral I had descended into. What could be worse than having nappies strapped to your legs as you went shoplifting to get drugs so you could get off your head. Every. Single. Day.

I owned no clothes, had no possessions, every penny that came into my hands was given to a drug dealer. I had no home, no family, no friends, no future.

As a definition of a down and out, that's it, isn't it?

At this point, I was starting to get nicked a lot. I was always horrendous to the police. I really hated them.

And they really hated me. They were just doing their job, but I was always causing them agg and being totally antisocial and disrespectful to them.

One day, like many others, I was arrested and taken to Romford police station.

The police officer at the desk laughed at me. 'We've got you this time.'

Unknown to me, they'd been following me with store detectives. I was in a department store and had picked up 10 leather jackets worth £200 each. I would have sold them for £500, which would have been enough money for my daily use.

As I ran out with an armful of jackets, I was jumped on by 10 uniformed officers and 3 store detectives.

I threw the jackets on the floor to try to escape, but there were too many of them. I couldn't run very well because my legs were in a bad way and I was weak.

It was quite late in the day, though, so when they took me to the police station to charge me, normally you went straight to court and were remanded in custody, but it was too late. The bus that took prisoners to court had already left, so I was told that I'd be spending the night in the police station cells.

I kicked off worse than usual because I was withdrawing from heroin in a bad way. They took me to the cell right at the back of the station and slammed the door.

Then they just started taking the piss:

'You're going to jail tomorrow.'

'Going to go cold turkey.'

I was sitting in the cell angry that I'd been arrested and desperate to get out for a fix.

I needed to escape which was, I know, virtually impossible. I was in a cell with two-inch thick walls. In a police station.

Still, I came up with a crazy plan which, if it worked, meant that I'd be out of the cell in a few hours, injecting. If it failed, I could die.

To get their attention, I started banging on the cell door. Really hard. Almost punching it, I was so wound up.

After half an hour, someone came and looked through the flap.

'What do you want?'

'I wanna have a shower. I haven't had one for weeks and I'm going to court tomorrow.'

An officer came round 20 minutes later, let me out of the cell and gave me a bar of soap and a white towel.

'Can I have a razor? I need a shave.'

The police officer took me to the shower room. 'I'll be back in five minutes. Hurry up.'

At this point I had no intention of having a shower. I had no intention of having a shave.

My intention was to slash my wrists.

I broke open the white Bic razor, stripped down to my underpants and slashed my wrist twice on each arm.

I don't remember feeling any pain, but I can still picture the blood gushing out of the arteries onto the white-tiled floor.

Then I heard a young voice screaming, 'Guv, he's cut his wrists! He's cut his wrists!'

I'd noticed a kid in one of the juvenile cells opposite the shower room. They'd left his hatch open; he'd seen me cut my wrists and the blood spurting all over the place.

The police officer came running in and pulled the curtain back.

'Call an ambulance.'

One policeman was retching and another came along with paper towels while a third shouted, 'We haven't got time to call the ambulance! He's bleeding to death!'

One officer put towels around my wrists and another tried to pick me up. They rushed me past the sergeant's desk. There were alarms going off and other officers rushing in from every door.

'What's going on?'

I was chucked in the back of a police car with one officer still guarding me. In the background, I could dimly hear the siren screaming as they sped through the traffic.

We got to A&E. At this point, I was starting to lose consciousness.

The next thing I knew, I was in theatre with doctors trying to pump blood into me.

But there was a massive problem: I had no veins left to use.

So they stuck a six-inch needle into my neck with a tube that went into my jugular straight to my heart. That was the only way they could get blood into me. I was panicking. This was the moment I could die.

Once they'd got the blood pumping into me, they started to look at my other wounds.

I ended up with 59 stitches in my wrists.

Four hours later, I was taken back to the police station and chucked into a cell again.

My plan had backfired. I was hoping after the suicide attempt that I'd either escape from the hospital or be let go under the Mental Health Act. I didn't think they could argue against the fact that I was mentally unwell and unfit to be in custody.

But there I was, four hours later, back in the same cell with bandaged wrists, humiliated.

As they threw me back into the cell, one of them said, 'You're still going to court tomorrow. You're going to jail.' I couldn't tell if he was laughing or not, but I was fuming – like properly lose-my-nut angry.

I casually stripped off and put all those disgusting drug addict clothes in the corner of the cell.

Then, totally naked, I squatted in the middle of the cell and did a huge shit on the floor.

I scooped it all up and smothered my body from the top of my head to my toes. Then I started to plaster it all over the walls, the door and even the hatch.

This time I pounded on the buzzer, kicking and punching the door as hard as I could with my bandaged hands.

A policewoman came to check on me. She was the same one who had driven me to hospital.

She pulled the hatch down, took one look and burst into tears.

When I think about what I must have looked like, I think I would have, too.

I was sitting there, a 30-year-old bloke, stark naked, smothered in my own faeces, 59 stitches in my wrists and holes in my legs. A total physical and mental mess.

And the whole cell stank of my shit too.

She cried, retched and ran to the panic alarm on the wall.

The siren started once again; everyone in the building came running. From the chief superintendent to the ordinary coppers, they all ran from wherever they were.

I could hear some of them gagging. One of them was definitely sick.

Some were swearing at me. They just couldn't believe that anyone could do that to themselves.

The whole of Romford police station were disgusted with what I'd done.

But now they didn't know what to do with me.

'Now,' I thought to myself, 'now I'm at the bottom of the spiral. I can't go lower than this, can I?'

I thought I was done. Broken. But clearly I wasn't, because it was still part of the plan to escape.

The policewoman came back. There must have been 20 officers outside the police cell door. She had got hold of a couple of doctors. And two psychiatrists came down from wherever they were on duty.

Everyone was really worried. Not only was this the act of someone who had lost their mind, but if I'd died in their cell, they would have failed in their duty of care and it would have been a huge problem for them.

They were really stressed about me but didn't have any idea what to do.

One policewoman, who I knew a bit because she was always picking me up for shoplifting, looked through the hatch. She had a tissue over her nose and mouth trying to keep the smell away (not just the shit, but the legs still smelt bad).

'Please, Paul, please have a shower and we'll let you go. Even though you've got a no-bail warrant we'll let you go.'

I washed, showered. Cleaned myself up.

I was taken to a room with six professional people including two psychiatrists and some senior police officers. For an hour they asked me a series of questions – analysing me, assessing how mentally unwell I was.

The police clearly wanted me to be sectioned, because they knew I was really mentally sick.

But over the course of an hour, I managed to convince these professional psychiatrists that I was OK, that I was well enough to walk out back onto the street, that I wasn't insane but just a drug addict.

I thoroughly answered every question they asked me, looking them in the eye, convincing the psychiatrist that I just had a drug problem but was otherwise mentally well.

The police were baffled.

My plan and my cunning had worked because just a few hours later I wasn't in prison and I wasn't in a mental asylum – I was out on the street, committing crime and going back to a crack den.

How was it even possible that that could happen? How could these five or six professionals not section someone who'd just done what I had? The bandages on my wrists, the shit that I'd had to shower off my body, the huge blood loss and violence. How was that not indisputable evidence of someone who needed help, who needed treatment for this illness?

I had escaped by manipulating these six senior professionals into believing that I was OK. But I was a homeless drug addict who had left school at 14.

They'd let me go knowing full well that I would be going straight out of the police station, committing crime and heading back to a drug den.

This illness, addiction, which is so powerful, so clever, almost genius in its levels of ingenuity, got me to talk my way out of this impossible situation. But I've come to realise that I'm just a vehicle for the illness. It works on you, controls you and makes you incapable of resisting it.

The police carried on nicking me when I robbed and banging me up, but they never gave up on me despite the fact that I was a nightmare to deal with and they had every reason to hate me.

Funny thing is that now, many years later, being clean and sober, I get invited back to the police station by the superintendent and other senior officers to do talks on mental health and addiction.

At that moment, though, I never in a million years thought that that would happen.

But I was back in the crack den with 59 stitches in my wrists, injecting crack and heroin into my groin.

The insanity of those years is hard to believe now.

CHAPTER FIFTEEN

From the time I smeared myself in my own shit and tried to kill myself to a moment seven years later when I finally gave up, life was a blur.

It continued in the same cycle that it had up until the shit-smearing moment with a few insane highlights. Or lowlights. I was either off my nut or in jail working the methadone programme.

All I did was nick my £2000 worth of stuff a day. Sell it. Get off my head. And start again the next day. I was injecting 50 or more times a day. A level of use that is beyond the imagination of 99% of addicts.

I tried to get sober a few times but really, I wasn't ready for it. Like everything else I did, I had to push my drug taking and desperate existence to within 0.1% of death.

And all the while, my health was taking a hammering.

My legs were a complete mess. I was dying.

Jewish Jim had vanished off the scene. I was struggling to walk. At all. With no car and messed-up legs, shoplifting was a massive problem. But I didn't have a choice. I had to get money to feed the crack monster inside me. I had to rob and fence so that I could live.

But with my legs so bad, just like the times in Ilford and Romford, a lot of crack dens wouldn't have me. It wasn't just because of the stink coming off my legs every time I took the nappies off. I was hard work. Always wanting more. They didn't want me close to them. I was trouble.

Imagine that just for a second: I'm being banned from going into the places where even dogs would hesitate to live, and the reason why I was rejected from many crack dens was not because I was violent or aggressive, it was because my using was way over the top.

The lowest of the lowlife who 10 years ago I was calling 'a scumbag junkie' wouldn't have me in their disease-filled, squalid flats. I became extremely lonely.

The illness of addiction took me to that point.

There are no easy cures for this. There is no silver bullet to get rid of the constant voice in your head saying that you have to inject.

I got sent to a rehab centre down in Salisbury, Wiltshire, as part of one of the many prison sentences I got during that time.

It was a brilliant place. An old stately home with great facilities and amazing staff. I got clean with the three-month programme.

I was then sent to a halfway house in Stroud. It was a dry house where you were meant to carry on with your rehabilitation, gradually start to put some pieces of your life back together: earn a bit of money, learn how to live the life of a functioning member of society – even pay bills and shit like that. (I didn't pay a bill until I was 38 – and it was a really surreal moment when I did.)

But I'd only been in the dry house a week when the call of the crack became irresistible. I went to an off-licence, bought some super-strength lager and jumped on the train to Romford.

Within a few hours, I was back in the only crack den that would take me. Injecting and getting ready to go out and shoplift again.

The thing about the shoplifting was that although my legs had healed up a bit during the rehab, they weren't fixed – still aren't – but the problem was not so much mobility now but the fact that every shop knew who I was.

I was a face that every undercover store detective knew like the back of their hand. I was the most prolific shoplifter in the United Kingdom. And how I was getting away with it – particularly in those high-end West End shops – was a complete mystery to me. I was a skinny, dirty-looking, smelly mess. I looked like I'd been dipped in glue and chucked through a charity shop window.

I was in one crack den – a new one – and just before they kicked me out, I was talking to a bloke who'd got nicked in Debenhams on Oxford Street a few days before.

The guy was chatting away about it, and then he pointed at me and started laughing.

'I don't believe it. I saw you in Debenhams.'

'You can't have done. Can't go in there any more.'

'I know. When they took me into the security office to wait for the police to come and get me, I saw your picture.'

'What do you mean?'

'Well, they had like a villains gallery on the wall. Snapshots of the well-known shoplifters.'

'So what? Don't all shops have that?'

'Yeah, but they had about a hundred mugshots, normal size and yours, yours was blown up to like A4. Couldn't miss you. And underneath it said: This is Paul Hannaford. If he comes in, just record what he's taking. Don't approach him. Just get the video evidence and send it to the police.'

I've got to admit I puffed up a bit then thinking that I was the most prolific shoplifter in London.

But that didn't help me get stuff to fence and money to buy crack with.

I had no driver, so I took to using cabs to go everywhere. Often I couldn't pay for them so had to keep switching from one firm to the other. Word got out – and in those days a lot of the cab companies were owned by the same people.

Even the police – despite showing some compassion in Romford – wanted as little to do with me as possible.

I got nicked one night in Romford. I'd tried to rob some clothes from a chain store but, with my legs, I didn't stand a chance of getting away. The shop manager called the police.

They turned up about an hour later, took one look at me and did that heavy sigh thing – you know, when your day's just got a lot worse.

They bundled me into the back of the van and the officer radioed into the local station:

'We've got Paul Hannaford here.'

The custody sergeant just said on the radio, 'Don't want him. Take him somewhere else. Make out that all the cells are full.'

They tried a few more before I got put somewhere about 15 miles away.

Even when I got there, they had to put two officers on me to make sure I didn't do anything overnight. One of the officers had to sit in the cell with me all night until I was taken to court in the morning.

The problem was that I was so unpredictable when I got to the station. And the stuff I'd done at Romford was well known to all the local forces. I just had a label that said 'too much trouble'.

By the age of 36, I was at the point where none of the cab firms would take me unless I paid up front.

Getting the £500 a day to buy the crack and heroin was becoming a proper problem. My profile was too high everywhere and my legs were giving out on me.

So how was I going to get drugs if I had no money?

At one point, when the gang was going strong, we got into fake guns. We never used them except as a threat when we were out grafting.

I had a fake revolver, which I never fired and which didn't have any bullets. When we got bored of using the guns, I buried it down Albert Road behind a fish and chip shop near my mum's house.

I went over late one night and started to dig. I found it among all the rubbish and worms wrapped up in three bin liners. A bit rusty, but it was still definitely a gun. And who was going to know whether it worked or if it was loaded?

As I unwrapped it, it did cross my mind about whether I should go and rob a bank or building society. But even though I was brave enough and desperate enough to have a go, I thought that it wasn't really my thing. I was a shoplifter and that was it. And I knew that if I went to rob a bank and get caught – which I would have done – I'd get 10 years. I didn't want to go in for that long.

It looked like a gun, and that's all anyone needed to know.

So, instead, I started robbing dealers with the fake revolver.

That was stupid as well, but it was also the most direct way to get crack and heroin.

These dealers were the people I was giving thousands of pounds a week to.

The first time I did it, I rang up Fabulous and arranged to meet him at Seven Kings – Ilford way.

I got a cab from Romford and as we got on the A12 to go to Seven Kings, around Gallows Corner, the taxi driver had been in the fast lane but pulled back into the slow lane. A police car – one of those that had armed police in way back then – came up in the fast lane, but then slowed down and pulled in behind us.

Bear in mind that I've got a fake gun in the footwell of the cab in a Tesco's plastic bag. It was 11 o'clock at night and there weren't any other cars around.

So I thought to myself, 'Shit, Paul, they're on to you. What're you going to do?'

My heart was in my mouth and racing like mad. I genuinely believed they were going to stop us, I'd be searched and that would be it.

The cab driver had no idea. He just thought he was taking a punter to some do or other, or home or to a mate's house.

So he carries on doing the speed limit with not a care in the world.

Meanwhile, in the back I'm shitting myself.

They followed us, right up our arses, for about two miles. And then they turned off at a junction.

But while I'm relieved, I'm still really nervous about meeting Fab because I've known him a long time. We're not exactly friends, but equally he's not a stranger and he's not an enemy.

I arrived at the meeting place but there was no one there. So I went to a phone box and tried him. No reply. I kept trying him but couldn't get through to anyone. I ran out of money to put in the phone and had to borrow some off the cab driver, after telling him that I was waiting to pick up some money from someone.

Finally, he turned up. I pulled the gun out and got him to hand over a huge bag of drugs. They were in total shock. It was completely silent. I had the drugs, but I was also aware that Fabulous wore a solid gold Rolex, which I wanted to take. That night, though, he didn't have it on his wrist.

I jumped back in the taxi which was around the corner and got him to take me to a crack den. When I got out of the cab, I told him that the guys had done me over for the money and could I owe him it.

He was, I think, happy just to get me out of the cab by that stage, as he knew I'd done something dodgy.

That was the first one I did. Fab wasn't happy and put the word out that he was going to get me.

But the most dangerous ones I robbed were the Ilford gang – brothers who had the market in that area sewn up. They had every addict on their books – making them £10,000-15,000 a day.

With them it was all crack and heroin. No weed. They might have had a different outlet for weed, but it isn't the most profitable drug to buy and sell. If someone buys a £10 bag of weed, it'll last them three days.

They loved my custom because I was spending £400-500 a day. Or I'd get a £10 lump of crack, do it in 10 minutes and come back for more.

I spent a lot of money with them.

One particular day I'd already spent over £500 with them, but come the night-time I wanted a bit more gear. But I didn't have any money, so I called them to see if I could get a bit of credit.

'No, you can't have any.'

'What? You're joking. I've just spent over £500 with you today. I only need £100 worth for the morning.'

'No, go and find some money.'

So I thought I'd do that. I got a train down to Goodmayes where they said they'd meet me at the Domino's Pizza by the station.

The reason they wanted to meet me there was because the oldest brother, M, wanted a pizza. He had a driver.

M was sitting in the passenger seat. His driver was acting like the runner.

I got into the back of the car.

'Have you got the hundred pounds?'

'Yes,' I said.

M handed a big bag over to the driver and told him to give me the drugs, and then M got out and went to get a pizza.

As the driver turned around to me, he said, 'Can I have the money?'

I pulled out my gun and stuck it in the driver's temple and said, 'Give me the whole bag.'

The blood drained from his face; he handed the bag over immediately.

There must have been about 200 cling film-wrapped balls of crack and heroin ranging from £20 stones to £50 stones. There must have been a good £5000 worth of crack and heroin in there.

It was in a Tesco's carrier bag, so when I got hold of it I said to myself, 'Sweet. I'm on a touch here.'

I jumped out. As I was doing that, M came out of Domino's with his pizza. The driver also jumped out. He was panicking because he'd just had a gun pointed at his head and realised that worse might come from M when they found out he'd given the drugs away.

The driver shouted out, 'He's robbed us! He's robbed us!'

M threw the pizza down, ran to the car boot and pulled out a massive wrench.

As he went to attack me with it, I saw that he looked behind me. Looking like he'd seen a ghost, he dropped his weapon on the floor.

I could see in the corner of my right eye a vehicle with an orange and blue stripe along the side panel.

It was the police.

A police dog van.

All I could hear was the dog barking like mad behind the grill in the car.

The two police officers in the front seats were heavily built. They wound down the window and asked M what was going on. I could only have been about a foot away.

At this point, though, everything was slowed way down in my head. I had a revolver on me and £5000 worth of class A drugs all bagged up and ready to sell – so I could never claim it was for personal use.

If they got out and searched me, I was in massive trouble. Carrying a fake firearm and having a huge stash of ready-to-deal class A drugs – that's a long prison sentence. A sign reading '5 to 7 years' flashed in front of my eyes. The judge and jury would never understand my level of drug use. They'd just write me off as a dealer.

And all I'd done was meet a dealer to get another fix. Again, this illness had pushed me into a situation where I could end up in jail for a long, long stretch.

Of course, M would deny everything, being a dealer or even having the drugs in the first place, so it was all on me.

But M was panicking as well. I don't know whether he had more gear in the car or what, but he really didn't want any bother with the police.

The driver could get a sentence, too.

'What's going on here?'

He could see it was kicking off.

M backed off, and I just said, 'It's all right. It's just a silly argument.'

I didn't know whether my heart was in my arse or my mouth, but I was begging them not to get out of the car. The dog, meanwhile, was going mad in the back of the car barking and foaming at the mouth. It could probably smell the drugs on me.

The policeman just said, 'Right, you go that way and you go that way.'

Pointing in opposite directions, he sent me down this alleyway to the side of Domino's, waited a few minutes and then drove off. To my complete relief.

When they pulled off, I ran as fast as my legs could take me.

I ended up in a crack den for the next four or five days and didn't move because I had enough gear to keep me going. That night, I think I took about a grand's worth of crack and heroin. Enough to kill most people, but I couldn't stop. I just wanted more and more.

The rumour started to circulate, though, that M and his family were looking for me. They had people out in their cars searching. Each of the cars had a can of petrol, a hammer and some six-inch nails in the boot.

When they found me, they were going to nail me to a floor somewhere, douse me with petrol and set me on fire.

It was a load of rubbish because I never saw them again. They just wanted to save face.

I ended up robbing all the dealers I'd ever bought from.

There were about seven of them. But it wasn't them who nearly killed me.

I'd arranged to meet the dealer one night, pacing around getting a bit nervous, not sure what was going to happen. He was also the only one I hadn't robbed, and I didn't know what I was going to do when I'd 'done' him.

The illness of addiction doesn't care about anything beyond the next hit, though, so getting more would be a problem further down the line.

His car pulled up and I jumped in the back. None of the dealers ever called my bluff about whether the gun was real or loaded or if I was prepared to use it. They valued their lives too much maybe or didn't care enough about the amount of drugs I'd taken.

I started to look in my pockets, apparently looking for money.

As soon as both the dealer and driver were looking towards the front of the car again, I pulled the revolver out and stuck it in the neck of the guy in the passenger seat.

The car was very quiet.

'Hand over the gear. All of it.'

They looked at each other. The main dealer – the one whose neck I was pointing a gun at – nodded.

'I'm going to reach forward and get it, Paul. Don't shoot.'

'Just hand it over.'

He bent forward and pulled out a bag of gear. I could feel the rush of the first hit already.

I grabbed the bag, waved the gun around and then opened the car door.

The driver looked over his shoulder as I climbed out and said, 'Jesus, Paul. You're in so much trouble now.'

I ran off to the nearest crack house I knew and opened up the bag.

Gold. There were lots of little balls of crack and heroin, but it also looked like there was a one ounce of heroin. It was about £1000 worth. They must have just bought it and hadn't yet had the time to cut it up.

It was a white colour, meaning it was probably pretty strong. Heroin is usually brown.

I had my normal fix.

The next thing I knew, I woke up in shock, naked apart from my underwear, with three paramedics leaning over me. They were sticking tubes down my throat and giving me CPR. I was dazed and had no idea what was going on. I passed out again, only waking up in the back of an ambulance with the sirens screaming and blue lights flashing.

CHAPTER SIXTEEN

I was taken back to Oldchurch Hospital, where they wired me up to every kind of monitor.

One of the paramedics told me that I'd been dead for two minutes but they'd saved my life with CPR and a defibrillator.

They took blood from my groin for a blood test. A little while later, a doctor walked up to my bed and pulled the curtain round. He looked concerned. 'I've got some bad news. You've got pneumonia, pseudomonas and septicaemia.'

I looked blankly at him.

'Pneumonia is a lung infection caused by a virus or bacteria. It can kill you. Pseudomonas is also an infection – you got that from injecting in your legs. It's not usually anything more than mild unless you already have an infection – like pneumonia – in which case it can get serious. And septicaemia is when you've got an infected bloodstream. It can be fatal.

'My diagnosis is that one of those things is going to kill you within forty-eight hours unless you let us treat you now. Your haemoglobin has dropped to four. Anything below thirteen point five is dangerous, but the number we want to avoid is three – when you die. You'll need a blood transfusion immediately.

'And we're going to have to amputate your left leg.'

As soon as he said I'd lose my leg, my first thought was how would I go shoplifting with just one leg.

I asked them where my clothes were. They said they were in a carrier bag under my bed.

The doctors left me. I was alone.

I quickly got dressed and walked out of A&E knowing full well that I would die in 48 hours.

But I needed to have a hit. Plus when I'd overdosed in the drug den, I must have left the big bag of gear I'd robbed. The other addicts would find it and I'd never see it again.

I hobbled round to collect it. Desperate.

I was wanted by the police for about three lots of shoplifting. Drug dealers were looking for me. I'd either get beaten to within an inch of my life if I was lucky or nailed to a floor somewhere and set fire to if I was unlucky.

I could barely walk because my legs were in such a mess.

And I'd just been told that I had 48 hours to live.

My body was finally giving up on me. The voice shouting 'get some gear' was loud, though.

And all the symptoms were coming on. I was sweating, couldn't breathe, was constantly tired and I couldn't focus. My legs hurt like hell and walking was becoming impossible.

I had to take my trainer off every hour to get rid of all the blood and pus that had drained into it from my wounds. It was like walking around in a waterlogged shoe, except this wasn't water.

The choice was finally in front of me: I was either going to die in a crack den or give myself up to the police.

I hated them.

As I hobbled along Romford High Street, wincing every time I put any pressure on my left leg, already desperate for another high, I slowly turned myself around and headed in the direction of the police station.

It took me half an hour to cover the ground of what was an easy five-minute walk.

As I stood outside, I remembered all the times I'd been in here. The arrests, the fights and the time I'd covered myself in my own shit and slit my wrists. Every single memory was bad.

I took a deep breath and walked through the automatic doors.

I limped up to the reception desk and looked at the sergeant. He looked me straight in the eye, bracing himself for a load of verbal from me.

I held his gaze for a split second, then whispered, almost begging, 'Please help me.'

And I collapsed on the floor sobbing my heart out.

I'd finally surrendered to changing my life. All the hate and anger and self-destructive thoughts and actions I'd had over the past 17 years had crushed me. They had made me into a shell of a human being – a weak, disease-ridden, infected, broken man.

When I was in hospital, no one came to see me. I had no friends, I'd robbed and alienated what family I had left, and my girlfriend and daughter had given up on me.

Alone, hated, broken, withdrawing and penniless, I'd run out of options. I had to throw myself at the feet of the police. It was a total surrender.

But I had just made the decision that saved my life. For once, I'd not hit the self-destruct button. I had stopped along the path towards certain death – a path that I'd managed to make much longer than most others – and I'd looked at a different route. One that took me back to life.

By this point, Ian, Peter and Russell had all died from drug overdoses.

The sergeant must have realised that I was close to the end. He raced around the desk and called some others. They picked me up, put me in the back of a car and blue-lighted me back to the hospital.

I received an emergency blood transfusion, they gave me shots of vitamin B12 to fix the low haemoglobin, a nebuliser for the pneumonia and they dressed my legs properly. I was in the high dependency unit (HDU) receiving critical care. For a couple of days it was touch and go whether I'd make it.

After three or four days, I could just about function again and my body was working enough so that my criminal life could catch up with me.

I was wanted in Romford, Southend and Chelmsford for shoplifting offences.

The hospital doctors put a wheelchair in the back of a police car and I was taken to Southend court on the fifth morning after I'd given myself up.

They wheeled me into court where I pleaded guilty to 19 counts of shoplifting.

The judge looked at me. 'Not you again, Mr Hannaford. I sentence you to six months for ten of the shoplifting crimes and six months for the other nine. Sentences to run concurrently.'

My last, I hoped, prison sentence was six months in Chelmsford prison.

The first person you see when you're taken to prison is the prison doctor. I arrived at Chelmsford having just come out of the HDU in hospital and, although my legs were dressed, they were not healed. There was still rotting flesh and open wounds.

The doctor took one look at them and said, 'You ain't coming to my prison. We can't cut your leg off. We don't have the equipment.'

So they took me in a prison van with three prison officers to Broomfield Hospital in Chelmsford to get my leg amputated. I was handcuffed to a prison guard all the way.

Even when I was admitted, the handcuffs stayed on.

The first doctor to look at me in Broomfield agreed. 'Yes, it's got to come off.'

They started to prep me for the amputation, and I was really panicking. It's only when you're faced with the reality of a situation like this that you realise the importance of things and all the damage I'd caused to myself.

I was pleading with them, begging them, to find another way of treating my rotten leg.

Eventually, I got another doctor to have a look.

He looked at the leg for a long time – it felt like an eternity – before saying some words that I never thought I'd hear: 'Let's try maggot therapy.'

I didn't know what to think of that. Maggots?

'Do you mean like insects?'

'Yeah, if you get them young, they eat the rotten flesh and the wounds can heal naturally and you can get skin grafts.'

'Does that mean the leg won't have to be amputated?'

'Well, we'll have to see if this works, but it's an alternative way of treating an injury like yours. Let's try it and see.'

He smiled at me and walked off.

I was relieved – anything had to be better than amputation, even though my leg was in a mess.

But I was still meant to be in jail, and I was doing my prison sentence in a hospital bed. The prison governor put six guards on me 24 hours a day – that were three shifts of eight hours each, two guards per shift. Basically, one guard would be handcuffed to me for four hours and then they'd swap. If I caused any agg, the other one would be there to help sort me out.

The handcuffs were on a 25-foot chain called a 'closet chain'. Whenever I went to the bath, the guards could come with me and stand outside the door. When I went to the toilet, I was in a special room and they fed the chain under the door.

The guards had a very cushy number and they knew it. They used to love coming to work because they just sat around and chatted all day.

For me, though, the maggots were becoming a reality.

A day or two after the doctor suggested the treatment, a nurse and a doctor approached with a vacuum pump and a jar.

They did what they call negative pressure therapy, which basically means they attach the vacuum to the wound and suck out all the gunge, pus and crap into a container so it can heal quicker.

The pain from that was horrendous. If you can imagine you've got an open wound, which is incredibly sensitive to any kind of touch, and then you start applying a sucking machine to it.

I was screaming. Even when they changed the dressings they had to hold me down, give me either something to bite down on or morphine or Entonox (gas and air). My legs were so painful that any kind of treatment or attention caused massive pain.

And after they'd used the vacuum, the jar with the maggots came out. In it were hundreds of tiny maggots, only a few hours old.

'I'll put about two hundred maggots in your wounds, wrap bandages around them and leave them for five days. They eat all the dead tissue and flesh away. And that should help your legs to heal.'

He poured on the maggots and fixed the dressings. It's the weirdest feeling you'll ever have. Your legs feel alive, but the living bit isn't part of you.

The maggots grew over the course of five days and got really big. Some of them escaped the bandages, and I'd wake up in the morning with maggots on my face.

It was disgusting, but I kept at it believing they were saving my legs.

I was now handcuffed in a hospital bed with maggots crawling all over me. If I thought my life had taken turns that I wasn't expecting, this confirmed it.

But the maggots saved my legs. And I went down to theatre about 10 times for skin grafts.

After about six weeks, or a quarter of my sentence, the treatment was still going on and the prison governor came to see me. I thought something serious had happened because he didn't do hospital visits.

It turned out that I was costing an absolute fortune. Keeping six guards on eight-hour shifts away from the prison, paying them overtime and taxis to and from the hospital was killing the prison budget.

So he said, 'I'm going to do you a big favour. I'm going to release you today on temporary licence, but you're not allowed off the hospital premises. You have to serve the remainder of your sentence in hospital. You're still a prisoner, but it's more like an open prison arrangement. You can't leave the hospital for anything unless it's a bit of fresh air, and that's for a maximum of thirty minutes. But we can't afford to keep twenty-four-hour custody watch on you. You're costing us too much money. Also, your trainers and tracksuit will be taken away and locked in the nurse's office so you can't escape.'

It would obviously save him a fortune but, if he knew me at all, which he should have, he must have realised this was a very risky plan. I may have had no footwear and clothes but that wasn't going to stop me.

They uncuffed me and the guards left. They were pretty pissed off because it was easier being in hospital than having to work at Chelmsford. And the overtime was paying for a lot of things. One of them told me that he'd got his summer holiday out of looking after me.

I really thought I'd had enough at that point. Addiction had taken me as far down as it possibly could – I was a shell of a person, my body wrecked and ruined, and my life in tatters. I thought I had nothing left.

But the illness wasn't finished. I had no defence against it.

Within 15 minutes, I was in a cab on my way to Chelmsford town centre, wearing an NHS gown, green foam NHS slippers, with a six-inch cannula CVC (central venous catheter) hanging out of my neck. What must I have looked like?

I'd just told the nurse that I was going out for some 'fresh air' like the prison governor had said I could. She said to make sure that I was back soon as I wasn't really allowed off the ward.

During the cab ride, it's more than possible that I passed the governor on the dual carriageway heading into Chelmsford!

When I got to the shopping centre, I told the cab driver to wait around the corner while I went in. Again, I can't stress enough what I must have looked like: hospital gown, no underpants, arse hanging out the back, NHS foam slippers, heavily bandaged legs and a huge cannula sticking out of my neck.

This is the reality of the power of this illness that is addiction. There it was in all its glory: a severely mentally unwell person walking through the streets of Chelmsford in a hospital gown and not much else, looking to rob money to get a hit, while not five days earlier he'd been watching the clock ticking down on the end of his life.

I ran into the nearest store without security guards and picked up over £1500 worth of stuff. I was only in there for about 10 seconds – in and out so quickly as always.

It still amazes me to this day that not one person, on the street, in the shopping centre or in the shops, not a single one, said anything to me. No one said, 'Excuse me, are you OK?' No one stopped me and said, 'Do you need any help?' Not one. I must have walked past 100 people from the cab to the store and back looking like I'd escaped from a secure unit somewhere.

Sometimes I think the public have to look at themselves a bit and ask why they don't just do a simple thing like ask someone if they're OK. It could make a world of difference to a person going through a terrible ordeal or through a bad episode.

Even the taxi driver didn't seem to bat an eyelid. Why are people so asleep?

I knew that as long as I was back before 5 p.m. when they served the tea, I'd be OK. So I had two hours to get to the shop, rob it, sell the stuff, buy some gear and get back to hospital.

The first two parts had gone off without a problem, but when I tried to find the fence, Mr T, he wasn't anywhere. I was still in the cab and out hunting for him but couldn't find him.

It got to six o'clock, by which time the hospital would have alerted the prison and the police, and I'd be flagged up as having absconded.

An APB (all-points bulletin) went out.

That night I sold the stuff and was back in a crack den, but I didn't have anywhere else to go. I managed to get some filthy dirty clothes to replace the hospital stuff.

I came out of the crack den the next morning and was walking down the road trying to get a taxi when three police cars pulled up next to me.

I tried to leg it as soon as they saw me, but they were too quick and took me back to Chelmsford nick.

I'd managed to push a whole load of needles under my bandages while I was in the crack den, so when I got back in prison, I got back on the crack. No one thought to search the dressings for gear.

All the work of six weeks getting sober and having treatment on my legs was thrown away.

The following morning they put me back on the prison bus, took me to the hospital and handcuffed me again.

And I was on the same routine for another six weeks until the sentence was spent.

While I was in hospital, visitors coming to see their friends and relatives would walk past, clock the handcuffs and the guards, and some started to chat.

'What you in for?'

'Theft. Ex-addict.'

And they started bringing me in fruit and chocolate. Over a period of a few weeks, all this stuff started to accumulate.

Even more so when I got MRSA in hospital, which was especially dangerous because of the state of my legs. I was getting through a bottle of Entonox a day.

At the end of the second period of six weeks, the prison governor came to see me again.

My sentence was up – I'd done three of the six months and I was free to go.

He unlocked the handcuffs, looked at me and said, 'I don't want you anywhere near my prison ever again. You've cost me a fortune – at least fifty grand. Stay out of trouble.'

And he walked off.

I rubbed my wrists, smiled at the guards and crawled out of bed.

The governor had bought my discharge grant, but the problem was that I had literally nowhere to go. If I left the hospital, I'd end up in a crack den and I'd probably die. I'd realised that no one had come to visit me, so I was on my own, with just one set of dirty clothing.

It was then that I finally understood I had no options left.

I had the £60 in my hand but if I walked out of the hospital, I'd probably be dead within a couple of days.

A nurse came in and said, 'Time to go. We need the bed.'

'I haven't got anywhere to go.'

'Well, you can't stay here.'

'Look, I've got no one on the outside I can go to. Literally no one, but I'm going to try and get properly sober. Can I give someone a call and see if I can get some help?'

She agreed.

My old addict mate, Lal, was in treatment in Somerset. I called him.

'Can you get me into rehab?'

'Not here, mate, but there is one that's NHS-run nearby. You may have some luck there. I'll call them for you, see if I can get you a bed.'

I asked the nurse if I could stay until Lal called me back. Again, she nodded.

Sitting around in the hospital, I realised I had to go for it this time. The other times I tried to get sober I had options. Now I had none at all.

Lal got back to me that evening and said, 'Yeah, there's a bed for you, but not for five days.'

'I ain't got five days.'

'It's the best they can do, mate. Hang on if you can.'

I had nowhere to go apart from another crack den. I was clean at that point. I explained to the sister that I had a rehab to go to, and she allowed me to stay until it was ready.

That nurse – with that one act of kindness – saved my life.

Every day I rang the rehab saying, 'Have you got a bed yet?'

'No, not yet. It'll be ready soon.'

On the day it was ready, I called the prison to get my travel warrant because they're responsible for getting you to a place once you're released.

I got my ticket to Weston-super-Mare.

I got a little holdall from the gift shop.

In it was a pair of shorts.

I had on a pair of West Ham shorts, a hoodie, my leg all bandaged and a dirty old pair of trainers.

And that was all I had to show for my first 37 years on the planet.

I hobbled out of the hospital on crutches, made it to the train station and got on. I left Essex behind not knowing when I'd be back.

When I got off the train in Somerset and had a look around, I thought it didn't look up to much.

Lal and his mate Albert picked me up at the station and took me to the treatment centre, which was two houses knocked together on an ordinary street.

But the moment I walked in there, it was such a relief. I felt that all the darkness and weight had lifted from my shoulders.

I'd found somewhere where there was hope. I felt like I was beginning to wake up.

That was February 2007.

CHAPTER SEVENTEEN

The first week was hell. I wanted to go back to Essex because it was all I knew, but at the same time I knew I'd die.

There was a calm, though, about the rehab centre that got to me.

I had my own room, my own space, which was pretty much the first time since we'd lived in the pub.

We had a lot of group therapy work, and for the first time in my life I was thinking about what I'd done to myself, to other people and to the communities I'd lived in. The focus on myself that wasn't just about the next hit.

My legs were still bad, so I had to walk down to the doctors every day to get the wounds dressed – they stank even after the maggots had had a go at them.

I had to go into hospital as well to receive more treatment for infections and when the dressings were really bad. And there were more operations. Over the course of my time in Weston-super-Mare, I had 11 skin grafts to help try to heal my legs.

The rehab was supposed to last six weeks, but with all the hospital visits and stays mine lasted ten.

After my first week of settling in, the idea was that you gradually started to do more 'normal' things so you could go into town, do some shopping and buy some food at Tesco.

The gym was no longer off limits, so I could go down there and do some weights when my legs weren't giving me grief. In that first period in the treatment centre, I managed to put on some weight.

The managers who ran the programme and the house were great, and I was in therapy with blokes I'm still in touch with: Paul, John, John and Katalina in particular. I go on holiday with one of the Johns now and I was invited to Kat's wedding in Santorini, Greece.

It made a massive difference to have the support of people who were going through the same process as you and who genuinely looked out for you.

I don't think I'd had that much attention paid to me for years – either by myself or by anyone else.

The basic daily regime was wake up around 7-7.30 a.m., have some breakfast and go into a group session. These sessions had different topics, but the idea was that it would be a daily reflection on some aspect of yourself or your life. We did some readings from the books on the course – they were spiritual.

The rehab programme was all about becoming spiritually awake. And that's really where the title of this book comes from.

I can't say much more about the programme other than it's step-based and I still use it, as do many others. We agreed to keep its specific contents between us, and I want to respect that.

What happened was that I gradually started to look at the damage I'd caused to myself, my friends, my family and my community.

It was hard. When you stop taking drugs and drinking and you wake up a bit, you think, 'What the hell have I done?'

But that's the shock of getting sober; your eyes start to open to a world outside your physical need to get high. You start to become aware, to become conscious of the world around you.

That's when the work really starts because the physical dependency is one thing, but repairing the mental damage and the hurt and pain you've caused others is another. And it's really hard to start that.

Part of the challenge is to start trying to make amends with the people you've harmed.

But all the time I cling to the thought that I'm still alive. Despite everything I've been through and done to myself, I'm alive and safe. I can feel the protection of the programme, and it comforts me.

Mentally, I've got a long way to go, but I've made a start.

Physically, my legs were still a massive problem. When one of the doctors at the hospital – Frenchay, outside Bristol – looked at my body, they reckoned by the end that I might only have had two main veins that could be used for anaesthesia for further operations. In the whole of my body.

The treatment was still agony. Every time I had to have the dressings changed, just like at Broomfield Hospital, the pain was unbelievable.

The doctors ended up trying to knock me out with morphine and Entonox so they could treat my legs without me screaming the place down.

I was nervous when they said they were going to do it because I thought that might count as a relapse, but on the rehab programme you're allowed medicines – even if it's morphine.

While they were treating the wounds, I got to move on to the next stage of rehab. That meant getting out into the community a bit more.

The programme, after you completed the first stage, lets you move out of the treatment centre into a flat or shared house. You still attend a session a week back at the rehab centre and all your individual meetings, but the idea is that you start to get some independence back.

It was a big mountain to climb, and I hadn't even reached the part where you have to move upwards.

The mental exercises were all about working on your ego, thinking about where your resentments and anger come from, and starting to let them go.

This was all stuff that I had ignored when I was doing crack and heroin. It meant nothing to me; it was all buried deep, as my life was all about the superficial physical high.

But my knowledge – the only thing I actually knew anything about – was drugs and crime. If I'd been asked to contribute to society by nicking stuff or cooking up heroin and crack, I'd have got a knighthood.

As it was, I didn't know about anything that would help.

This was something that I would only gradually remedy over a number of years.

But when I got out of the first phase of rehab in 2007, I was a shell, but I wanted to be better. That was the important thing. I'd got to the end of the line with drugs and crime, and now I was on a path to find out more about myself and what I could do. I had to learn how to live life again.

As I was moving on to the next stage, a guy called Nicky arrived from London. We clicked straight away.

Four of us moved into a shared house. Each with our own room. It was called a dry house, and we had to support each other to keep clean and sober.

It was brilliant. In total there were seven of us, and sharing a house was a laugh. I hadn't had mates like that since being in the gang, and we got on as though we'd known each other for years. I guess we all had so much in common from our years of using.

While I was taking the first steps to improving my mental health and the social side of my life was getting better and stronger, my body wasn't.

My legs just wouldn't heal. By 2008, they were in a real mess.

The doctors had tried skin grafts, especially on my left leg, but they didn't work properly.

Normal skin grafts take skin from another part of your body and it's applied to your wound in the hope that it will start to grow. The problem is that the rate of rejection is really high.

After the operation, you have to stay in bed for four or five days. If it doesn't take – and I think at least 30% has to 'take' before they call it a successful operation – you're back to square one.

In fact, you're worse off because each time they do a graft, the wound gets slightly bigger because before they do the operation they do something called debridement, which is cutting the dead skin away from around it.

So, the wound on my left leg was actually getting bigger.

I was spending three months in hospital at a time. My body was deteriorating and my mental health was getting worse and worse. It was hard enough dealing with rehab and following the programme and keeping clean and sober when you're physically fit.

If you're physically falling apart, it's a total nightmare.

I'd had nine or ten grafts, but with no success.

People were coming to visit me – which made a change – but I was getting bedsores and feeling really frustrated.

I'd even started looking up prosthetics and had said to the doctor that I wanted my left leg to be amputated. I just couldn't stand another graft. I would rather, at that point, have got rid of the leg altogether.

'Cut it off. Please just get rid of it. It's too painful. I'd rather be rid of it. I'm done with it. I've been in and out of hospital for years with it. It's getting worse. I've got no quality of life. Get rid of it.'

They took me seriously. Something I wasn't used to either; no one takes addicts seriously. And I had a long assessment meeting with a psychologist to make sure I was sane enough to make the decision in favour of amputation. He sat with me for about an hour and a half asking me all sorts of questions about everything – some of them really random, which I think were meant to throw me off my guard.

The psychologist's report came back and said that I was mentally fit to make the decision. I was relieved. After all that waiting around, anticipation and disappointment, and all that pain, the thought of not having to deal with it again was exciting. I thought that at last I could move on.

Then I got a visit from a doctor. He was Scottish and called Dr Reid.

'I'm not doing the amputation.'

I was fuming.

'You're joking? I've just had approval from the psychologist and I don't want to go through another graft. It's a nightmare lying here in bed for months on end. I want to get on with my life now.'

'I know, but there's a new treatment that I think will work for you. I think I can sort it.'

They'd just started an operation called a stem cell graft. Basically, they take a biopsy of your leg – this involves taking four or five layers of skin, which would be fascinating if it wasn't so massively painful. But you can see the cells way below your skin, which is amazing.

They send the biopsy off to a lab, and in three weeks it comes back as a graft – a disk, in my case – that can be placed on the wound. They grow your own skin for you.

The first time they did it, my body rejected it. Again. I was raging.

My haemoglobin count was low still, which meant that my immune system couldn't cope and rejected the graft.

Again, my mental health went way down. It crashed after that. So they sent me back to the house with dressings on my legs, which I needed to get treated every day to prevent infection.

I needed to get out of hospital and see my mates again in my own room before I went back in for another go. I had a week's freedom before I went back in.

This was late in 2008.

My left leg was the really difficult one. I was on warfarin, but I kept getting DVT because I was lying around so much in hospital beds.

And then I got really badly dehydrated. I was getting more ill in hospital than I was out. But it was the only place for me to be. The pain was still horrendous: if they touched my leg, I'd pass out.

Stem cell treatment is expensive, but I think I had another 10 treatments over the course of months and months before finally a graft got to 20% acceptance and slowly started to grow.

It was really slow. And 13 years later, it's still not 100%. And my right leg suffered because they were taking skin from that to grow cells for the left leg.

When the graft finally took and I left hospital, my time at the dry house had come to an end.

I managed to get a one-bedroom flat.

It's difficult to describe my emotion when I unlocked the front door for the first time. From my childhood ups (home, the pub) to downs (getting kicked out of the pub and having to go with my stepdad and mum) to adult moments of peace (with Joanne and her mum) to years of living like a dog (crack houses and the streets), this was a moment that I could hardly have dreamt of a year before.

I felt proud of myself for having got that far, excited about what might be coming down the road and determined to try to make amends for the harm I'd caused.

Increasingly, my meetings and reflections on my life had come out in a phrase that I'd learnt during rehab. It's the first thing I say to myself every morning and the last thing I say at night.

I've never been a reader and I would never have come across this phrase if it hadn't been in one of the books in the programme. It comes from Shakespeare:

Love all, trust a few, do wrong to none.

The first and last points are the most important to me.

As I turned the key in the door to a flat on Jubilee Road in Weston-super-Mare, I had this sense of being human.

I walked in and saw a sofa that wasn't covered in blood spots, a carpet not littered with needles and used syringes, and a kitchen with pots, pans, plates and spoons – none of which were blackened by cooking up gear.

It felt immaculate, just like I had all those years ago when I used to go to the pub and be dressed properly.

This was my place. I had keys and could do what I liked. There was no one shooting up beside me, no danger of an angry dealer turning up or the police knocking down the door.

The flat was my place of calm.

I loved it.

After a few weeks, I got a letter. I was excited. I opened it up and it was a gas bill.

That made me so happy. I was 38 years old and had never paid a bill in my life. I stared at it. It felt like a passport to a new life.

Then the reality hit me that I hadn't got a clue how I was supposed to pay it. I had money, but I didn't actually know what the process was!

Someone who had been around a while in recovery explained it to me. The next day I went to the post office beaming like I'd just won the lottery and paid my first ever bill.

CHAPTER EIGHTEEN

As I carried on with rehab and dealing with my rotten legs, I was surprising even myself.

Looking for stuff I could do as a job, because, like I say, all I knew was drugs and crime and I had no school qualifications at all, I decided to sign up with a TV extra agency in Bristol.

They found people who wanted to be on screen as bit-part actors.

I was, and still am, easily cast as a tough guy, a hard man, because of the way I look.

Anyway, I signed up with them and started to get a bit of work as a thug or a villain.

I ended up getting small parts on EastEnders, Doctor Who, CBBC and Casualty, always playing the villain, which meant that I didn't have to act much.

One weekend I was on Casualty and had to play a gang member in a drug den. My only thought was that this was very, very easy. The director was really pleased; he told me how authentic I was.

And I laughed to myself. Little did he know that I'd been rehearsing for this part for the past 20 years.

I just said, 'Yeah, well, I've seen a few things in my time.'

'You're good at this, though.'

The agency agreed. I was getting auditions – this was in 2009 – and seemed to be in demand. I was travelling up and back to London trying to land jobs in adverts or tiny parts in TV dramas. Always playing the criminal.

But because my reading isn't great – not just from the drugs, but also because of my ADHD and because I left school so young and never completed my education – I found reading a script for an audition or in front of directors really difficult.

Add to that the fact that I wasn't a trained actor and, while I was getting the auditions, I wasn't landing many parts.

The guy at the extras agency said to me, 'You've got the right look and can do it, so why don't you get some acting lessons? It'll improve your chances of getting the parts and it might give you some confidence that you really can do it.'

My time in Weston-super-Mare was gradually coming to an end anyway. I'd been in my one-bedroom flat for about a year and the lease was coming up for renewal.

It was time to make a decision about the future. I had started to wake up in Weston – the programme had made me aware of what I had done and what I was doing. It set me on a path that I'm still following today.

But I realised that I couldn't progress further without confronting some of my old life. I had to deal with it at some point, even though I was worried as hell about it.

When the guy from the agency suggested getting some acting lessons, it planted a seed. I thought that perhaps I should go back to London, face up to my past and try to start something new there.

I did some research online looking up 'method acting'. To be honest, I didn't really know what I was doing, but I'd heard of it so I thought that was a good place to start.

The search got me in touch with this guy called Sam. He was an ex-actor who ran courses of different lengths. He took on people with no experience as well as those who had done some acting.

I took a chance and contacted him.

We had a chat and he encouraged me to sign up.

It was a big moment. If I decided to commit to it, I'd be moving back to Essex and all the old places full of memories of my old life. Was I strong enough to go there? Who would remember me? Would the triggers I got there from the people and places put my rehab in danger?

Going back to where you started is an important part of what we do on the programme. It's really there that you can start to make amends, to try to make up for the harm you've caused.

But it was going to be tough to do that. A massive challenge – one that could put my whole recovery in danger.

Added to which, I'd been in touch with my dad. He was dying. I wanted to go and see him, but I thought that the happy memories of my childhood and the fact that I still worshipped him as my God would be too much for me to deal with.

I didn't go when I had the chance. Dad died before I got to see him. I was absolutely devastated. I went to the funeral, and that was the first time I'd been close to him since I was 11 years old. It was a very hard time and very hard to deal with.

Hopefully he's in Heaven today looking down on the new man I am.

I got a place in Hornchurch, the scene of some of my extreme childhood memories, and started on a 12-week intensive acting course with Sam.

It was one of the hardest things I've ever done. I had to step so far out of my comfort zone trying to be other people and do things that I could never do. I was exhausted at the end of each day.

I left after eight weeks. It wasn't for me. I was grieving and confronting my past – the emotional rollercoaster was too much.

Meanwhile, though, I was still in the programme. There was support in Essex, so I carried on my meetings there.

I also started to do some open mic gigs. I found that my cheeky, smiley personality had come back a bit, and I was popular at them. And I had so many stories to tell that I had a bit of an audience. People would gather round when I was talking.

At one of them, an organiser of a drugs convention asked if I'd do a half-hour introduction to open the conference. I stood on stage, told my stories and went down a storm with the 1000 or so ex-drug addicts and counsellors.

The invitations started to pile up and before I knew it, I found myself doing some stand-up comedy at open mic nights around London.

The gigs were never paid. I just did them because I was good at it and, at the beginning, I enjoyed it. Here I was, a kid who had left school at 14, who had gone on a massive self-destructive journey, taking a load of people with him; a kid who'd nicked millions of pounds' worth of goods from shops all over south-east England, who'd been to prison 10 times, who'd been stabbed five times and died twice; a kid who'd taken more drugs in 15 years than whole cities would in the same time. Here I was on stage making people laugh about life.

It was surreal.

I thought it was going quite well and that I might have a bit of a future. Doing just a bit of the course was enough to give me some confidence onstage and I had an endless supply of material.

I had a good run of gigs, and then five or six that weren't that well received. I don't know whether it was me – whether I was getting bored – or whether the audiences were off, but it made me realise what a tough gig stand-up is. And there were, at the time, still are, hundreds of great comedians, much better than me, doing it, so I thought I'd leave them to it.

Every step I took in Essex reminded me of my past.

The flat I had in Hornchurch was opposite a school.

One morning, I woke up with an idea in my head. I watched, every day, as kids streamed into the school for assembly and their education.

My idea was that I should try to tell them about what happened to me. About how I didn't finish my education, what a mess I had become, and about the dangers of drugs and alcohol, of gangs, of crime and knives.

After all, I'd lived it and only just managed to make it through. If I told them the truth behind the rubbish they hear on social media and from mates, if I helped them to understand the reality of the consequences of having your first hit of heroin or leaving school early or getting into crime, then perhaps I could stop a few from following me down the same path.

But I knew I just couldn't walk into a school and ask at reception if I could do it. I knew I needed some sort of official introduction, be part of a scheme or get support from the education department somewhere. I had to be credible.

I got in touch with the local council to organise a meeting with the drug and alcohol team. It was the only way I could think of to break into the official channels. I told the guy my story.

He listened respectfully, which I thought was a good start.

'It's not my decision, though. It's my boss's. He's away this week. Back next week. I'll talk to him then.'

I went back the following week. The boss was now off sick. I went back the next week; he was in a meeting. The fourth week he was off on holiday again.

After turning up for the fifth week and not getting another meeting, I think they thought they'd got rid of me. They probably thought they'd never see me again.

But I kept turning up. Once I get an idea in my head, once I have a plan, I don't give up.

Week after week I appeared at the council offices.

In the end, I got another meeting. If you want to get something done, you have to go and be there physically. If you phone or email – as I found out again and again – you're too easy to ignore.

I sat in a room with three people from the department. They had no idea who I was, I didn't have any pictures of my injuries and my story wasn't that coherent or well told. I had no website, no endorsements from anyone, no presence on social media – I was just some guy who'd taken drugs but was now recovering. They must have seen that all the time.

But I went through it anyway, and at the end I asked whether I could do some unpaid voluntary work. Try to put something back into a system I'd taken so much from.

'OK. Leave it with us.'

About a week later, I got a call from the first guy I'd seen – Darren. He said there was a youth club in Rainham, Essex, that thought a few of the boys could benefit from a chat with someone like me. Did I want to go along?

Of course I did.

It was a hot Monday night in June 2010. Darren picked me up from my flat in Hornchurch and drove me to the club.

There were about 10 or 15 kids sitting around or playing pool and table tennis.

Chris, the guy who ran the club, stood up as I walked in.

'Right, everyone, stop what you're doing and come and sit down.'

I could see them thinking, 'Who's this guy and why are they interrupting our time to play and muck about?'

But I just started to chat, and we ended up talking the rest of the night. I just sat there and told them all about what I'd done, and they had lots of questions.

I left feeling pretty good.

Four days later, I got another call from Darren. 'One of those kids you spoke to went back to his school and told his head teacher about you. The head wants to know whether you can come in and do an assembly for a year group.'

'How many kids?'

'Two hundred and fifty.'

'What, a big assembly like that?'

'Yeah.'

'All right, then.'

So I've now got to go and tell my story to a group of 250 kids without any props or pictures or anything.

I did the assembly and the head loved it. He said, 'Can you speak to the whole school? And by the way, my wife's a head of another school in Hertfordshire. She's interested. Can you talk to her too?'

That's how the school thing started. It was all from one idea and a lot of persistence. Fair play to the council for making it happen as well.

The requests started to come in. I'd be asked once or twice a month to travel to a school – sometimes it was to talk to the older year groups, sometimes to the whole school. I realised that some days I spoke to 1000 or more kids.

The numbers started to rack up that autumn and into the winter of 2011. The drugs and gangs stories kept appearing in the press, and it was obvious that the police and government were under pressure and something needed to be done.

The ambition started to form in my head that I'd like to speak to one million kids, telling them about what I'd done and how I'd only just survived. I'd show them my legs, the syringes and needles, the crack dens, and tell them about my old mates in the gang – many of whom aren't here today.

My presentation developed: I took along photos and props.

And then another idea hit me.

My dream as a kid was to play for West Ham. I'd lost that dream when I started to take drugs. There must be thousands of kids who had similar dreams, though – and football clubs now had academies that looked after children from the age of eight or nine. And they had massive influence in their communities.

I emailed all the clubs in the Football League – from Manchester United to Rotherham and Dagenham and Redbridge. Every single one. There was no way I could go and camp out at their offices, so I had to resort to a blanket email.

None of them got back to me. They didn't know who I was, so why would they?

So I built a website. I had some pictures, a rough version of my story and I added some feedback I'd received from teachers. It was basic, but at least I was there on the internet for people to see.

A few months later, I was still giving talks in schools and at the occasional youth club, I received an email from a guy called Gareth at QPR in west London.

> Hi Paul
> Got your email. Sounds interesting and could be beneficial for our academy players and also the kids we help in the local community.
> Would you like to come in for a chat?

I jumped at this chance. I caught the train and tube to west London and met a bunch of guys there who manage the community side of the club. They took me into one of the corporate hospitality boxes to talk about what I had done, what I was doing and what I would be prepared to do.

I told them my story and showed them pictures of my injuries. I spent two hours with them.

'We're sure your talks will have a positive impact on the kids in our community. We'll be in touch.'

I left the stadium on a high. Later that evening when I was back home and still buzzing from the meeting, I got another call from QPR.

'Paul, we've got ten talks we'd like you to do. It's part of the Kicks project run by the Premier League.'

Kicks started in 2006 and it aims to help kids in some of the most high-need areas to get involved in sport. It started with four clubs, but now 90 Premier League, English Football and National League clubs participate.

QPR wanted me to focus on the physical and mental well-being, and to help the kids walk away from the temptations of drugs, gang culture and knife crime. The whole idea was like mine – to help children avoid the mistakes I'd made, to help them make better choices and to show them that there's a whole world of stuff they can do with their life.

How cool is that?

I was getting better at promoting myself and thinking more about how I could establish what I do. So I asked if I could put the QPR logo on my website. They agreed. So now I had a brilliant brand on the site as well as an endorsement from them.

At one of the Kicks sessions, one of the QPR media guys videoed me and the kids talking.

A few weeks later, Gareth invited me to a game against Sunderland. It was live on Sky Sports.

They told me they'd take some pictures and do a write-up about it in the programme for the next game. That excited me.

I turned up. Watched the first half – it was great to be back inside a football ground after all those years (and very different from West Ham in the 1980s).

At half-time, when I was looking to get a burger from the buffet, Gareth said, 'We've got a surprise for you.'

They took me down to meet Anton Ferdinand and another player who brought me down from the box to the pitch.

I walked to the centre circle with a few of the officials, and there was a club photographer snapping away.

It was a childhood dream come true. Here I was at the centre circle of a major football club being recognised for the important work I do.

Gareth pointed to the big screen above the goal and said, 'Have a look at the screen.'

And there I was. They were playing the video from a few weeks back showing me educating the kids on the Kicks project. At half-time of an English Championship match. In front of 20,000 fans.

'This is incredible.'

I welled up. It felt like such a massive moment – almost as though I was reconnecting with the kid who wanted to be a footballer.

I got a huge reaction from that. A few weeks later, Reading Football Club got in touch and I did the same thing there.

A guy called Tommy at Millwall got in touch. He was part of their community team. He invited me to the stadium to talk to local kids. Over a couple of years, I must have spoken to thousands of them.

It felt like I had some momentum behind me.

Then other opportunities came up. I got an email from the London Fire Brigade.

> Dear Paul
> We run a course called L.I.F.E. It's for schoolkids who come to a fire station for a week and we teach them life skills. We haven't got any money, but would you be willing to do one or two talks for us next week? If they work out, it might be possible to get funding for more talks.

I said yes immediately.

The first talk I gave was at Bexley Fire Station, followed by another at Dagenham.

They went down a storm. Then I got a follow-up email saying they had 20 more events they wanted me to do. And they'd found some money to pay me as the talks had been received more positively by the young people than anything else they'd done.

A few months later, I was invited to an awards ceremony where the commissioner presented me with an award for my work on the L.I.F.E. course.

I was asked to attend another awards ceremony at Lord's Cricket Ground. There, the head of Barclays Spaces for Sports presented me with the Street Chance award for the drugs and knife crime talks I did with QPR. If you'd told me that at any point during my addiction, I'd have laughed.

After that, things went a bit mad. Manchester United invited me to give three talks in two days.

Kicks organised a tournament at Hackney Marshes. I did a workshop there. There were 20 kids from every single club in the country – 900 or so children – and it was covered by Sky Sports.

Football, the fire brigade, schools and youth clubs were all knocking on my door.

Two or three years after I gave that first talk in Rainham, I'd been to every Premier League club and a lot in the lower leagues as well.

Things were really taking off. I wasn't being paid very much as a lot of it was unpaid, but that didn't matter as I was thoroughly enjoying giving my talks.

To top it all off, I got a call from the police community team to go to Romford police station and speak to representatives of the local authority and senior police officers about the work I was doing and how we could stabilise or reduce harm in the borough. This was something I never thought would be possible.

And to think, all those years ago, I was in that same police station, causing absolute mayhem by covering myself in my own shit and cutting my wrists. Now I had an opportunity to be a pillar of the community rather than a burden.

I didn't leave anything out. There were a few tears that night, I don't mind admitting.

CHAPTER NINETEEN

This last chapter on my life is about family and the future.

Since I was forced to leave my dad and started on my years of self-destructive drug taking, I have managed to devastate my family. Both the family I was born with and then the family I made.

I stole my mum's jewellery – including her wedding ring – when I robbed her house to get money for crack and heroin. That same night I nicked my brothers' PlayStations and Xboxes. I didn't care what damage I caused; I needed to feed my habit. I needed a fix and that was all that mattered.

I didn't see my mum much. And when I hit rock bottom I hid myself away. Now, bless her, we meet once a year on my birthday in a café and she gives me a birthday card. That gesture means the world to me.

When I was with Joanne and staying at her mum's house, I used it like a hotel. I walked away from Joanne when she was about to give birth to my daughter.

In those years growing up, it seemed for a while that my family was first the gang and then any addicts I hung around, injecting with.

But in rehab, I looked at my life through different eyes. I saw what I'd done to the people who I should love.

When I moved back to Essex and started the school talks, Joanne's mum, Kay, sent me some pictures of Ria so I had an idea what my daughter looked like.

One Saturday afternoon in Romford, I was sitting having lunch in a pie and mash shop – the same one, funnily enough, where Joanne and I had our first date.

I was eating away not really thinking about much, when I looked up and saw Ria standing in the queue not 20 feet away from me. I was stunned – she was beautiful – and I tried desperately not to stare.

A couple of minutes later, she was joined in the queue by a man about my age. I realised he was her stepdad. The guy Joanne had ended up with. They must have been out shopping together and were stopping for some food.

The thought flashed into my mind that it should have been me doing that.

But as quickly as that thought entered my head, I also knew that I didn't deserve the privilege of taking my daughter out. I had chosen drugs instead.

I got up and left the restaurant feeling absolutely gutted – it was the hardest, toughest reminder of what I'd missed out on and what addiction had done to my life.

I also realised that I had to respect my past and appreciate that this man, her stepdad, had done a better job as a dad than I could have.

A few days later via my website, I received an email from a teacher at an all-girls school in Upminster, Essex. The school was called Sacred Heart. Kay had told me that this was where Ria went.

The email asked if I'd do a talk on alcohol and drugs to the Year 10s. Ria was in Year 10. I accepted but thought I'd better let Joanne know that I would be going.

I called her expecting the worst, but she was quite pleasant with me. She'd heard that I'd started to sort my life out and was giving back to the community.

Unfortunately, Joanne said Ria was doing work experience that day so wouldn't be in school.

I was very disappointed.

But a week later, I went and gave the talk anyway, which the Year 10s liked. I left at lunchtime and started to walk back to where I was staying. I looked up, and there was Ria walking towards me.

My heart started to pound. I had a matter of seconds to pluck up the courage to say hello.

I stopped in front of her, put my hand out and introduced myself.

'Hi, Ria. I'm Paul. I'm your dad.'

She hugged me.

I was blown away.

We chatted for about five minutes, but she had to get back to school.

As soon as I got home, I wrote her a letter to explain why I had let her and her mum down so badly and that I wanted to make amends for it all. The letter took me most of the day. I can't spell and had to google most of the words because I didn't want her to have a bad impression of her dad.

The letter explained about my past life of drug addiction and alcoholism, my involvement with gangs and, therefore, why I could not be a responsible father.

I put my address and phone number at the bottom so she could contact me.

The letter was 10 pages long.

I asked her to forgive me.

And said I would love to see her again.

When I sealed the envelope and put the stamp on, I was so excited.

I put it in the postbox and prayed that she would contact me.

Two or three days later, the postman came but there was no mail. I checked my phone hundreds of times a day for a week. No text.

After a week I thought, 'I know what I'll do, I'll send her a friend request on Facebook.' I sent it. Nothing. No reply.

At the end of two weeks I thought, 'That's it. She's obviously decided she doesn't want to see me.'

I was absolutely heartbroken. Gutted. But I said to myself, 'Why would she want to see me? She's got a dad and I wasn't there for her or her mum. I chose drugs. Life goes on.' I was very sad but couldn't do anything about it.

The next day my phone rang. It was Joanne.

'What's wrong?' I said.

'Nothing. We just got back from holiday last night. We've been away for two weeks. Ria's read your letter this morning. Would you like to take her out next week for something to eat? She was upset but inspired by your letter. As was I, Paul.'

At this point, I had goosebumps all over my body and thought to myself, 'Did I just hear that right?'

'Yes. I'd love to.' I had a massive smile on my face as I said it. That phone call gave me a bigger high than any drug I'd ever taken. Because it was pure and loving.

A week later, I arranged to meet Joanne and Ria in Romford; I was so nervous it was incredible.

Joanne met me with a hug. And then so did Ria. Joanne left us to it and we trotted off together.

I took my daughter off for a cheeky Nando's where we sat for hours talking, with me doing my best to explain my past life and why I couldn't be a responsible father.

And now I see her all the time. She tells me she loves me and gives me great big Father's Day cards. I take her out shopping on a Saturday when she's free. She's left school now and has a job. I'm so proud of her. I talk about her to the students I see in schools up and down the country. She suffered because of my drug and alcohol abuse.

When schoolchildren see what I missed out on, what I turned my back on, it makes the point really powerfully about the damage drugs can do.

Without this rubbish in my life that killed all my mates and nearly killed me, nearly, I'm a good dad.

We're meant to make our family proud, aren't we?

It's not just family who have suffered. I've explored every avenue of addiction, drugs, alcohol, violence, prison time, near-death experiences – from overdoses to being stabbed. I know all about homelessness and living in crack dens. I know about battles with the police and about the dangers of taking on drug dealers. I know many drug users, addicts and criminals.

If there's a dangerous situation to be in, I've been there. Like I say to a lot of people, I've got a PhD in Human Misery. I know all about it.

So as part of my recovery, I started to take an inventory of my life. I knew I needed to make amends not just to all the people who I've harmed in my life, but to myself as well. I'm still learning about that all the time; every day I understand something new.

A lot of my recent understanding is around the idea of being free. I can see that I'm getting myself clear of all the 'material goods' thinking. Free from the expectation that we're brought up with – to be successful you have to have stuff, new stuff, all the time.

What matters is what's inside, so that's what I'm focusing on, every day.

I also stopped taking myself so seriously. That has set me free. I stopped taking life so seriously as well, and that has given me freedom. I realise that although what I do is important, I, as an individual, am not that important. I'm a messenger and it's the message that's important.

The way I live now is summed up by a tattoo I have on my arm where I can see it clearly every day:

Love all, trust a few, do no harm.

It's based on the quote from Shakespeare mentioned earlier.

The words were told to me by a friend called Nick who I met in recovery. When I started to think about harm and then googled it, I found that it's attached really strongly to fear. So much harm comes from fear.

When I joined the gang all those years ago and we started doing the alcohol, the drugs, being violent and committing crime, I think I knew that it was harmful to me and others, but because I'd defined myself, my ego, as being outside of what society calls normal, I was afraid to change that perception of me. I was afraid of doing something different from what I'd become by joining the gang.

One other aspect of recovery that has been so important to 'waking me up' is being emotionally honest. It's hard. In fact, it's much easier to be emotionally dishonest, but that is an act of self-harm too. By not being emotionally honest, you're not respecting yourself.

Nowadays I live a decent life. I'm very conscious of myself, the world, life, my environment and the people in it. And I'm alive to the way I think, the way I act, the way I feel. I focus on the today.

For me, now, life is all about consciousness and spirituality.

I don't drink, take drugs or smoke. As I write this, I'm 13 years clean and sober. I can fix myself without needing any of the things I used to do. What other people do doesn't bother me. I know hundreds of drug addicts and criminals – but I don't do what they do any more. And what they do is none of my business.

I have very few jobs to do every day – wake up, stay clean and sober, and reach out and try to help someone. That's it.

A lot of the messages I receive on social media after I've given a talk at a school assembly are 'you woke me up'. I think it's important to see that telling the truth from first-hand experience is massively effective if we want to solve this problem that we've got in society.

What's the opposite of being awake? Being asleep…my job is to wake them up.

There are barriers to this. A lot of head teachers don't understand the real nature of the behaviour of drug addiction, alcoholism and gang life. And I totally get it's a head teacher's job that all their students receive the best academic development the school can offer. But we need, as a society, to give every child workshops around personal well-being.

My recovery has taught me a lot about other people and about myself. I live my life fearlessly now: I don't worry about anything other than keeping clean, sober and doing no harm to anyone. So my life is calm and clear. It's decent. I'm really conscious of me, the world I live in, my life, my environment, the people in it. The way I think, the way I act, the way I feel.

I don't let things bother me in the way that I see so many people battling every day. I'm not the angry, violent kid who wanted to prove to himself and everyone around him that he could take the most drugs, or drink the most cans of lager or commit the most crime. I have peace and a way of going through life that keeps me content and mindful of what I've got with no expectation of getting more.

When I go to my group meetings for my recovery, I meet people there who have all suffered at some point in their life, and it's great to see them all reaching out to help each other stay clean and sober.

Every morning I wake up and do a little personal inventory of my life: I'm clean, I'm grateful. I'm sober, I'm grateful. I have a job, I'm grateful. I have a roof over my head, I'm grateful. I have my daughter in my life, I'm grateful. And my mother, who must have suffered terribly and no longer does, now has peace of mind, I'm grateful.

I still have to dress my legs even though I'm nearly 14 years clean and sober. I still have a needle stuck in my arm and 14 blood clots, so I'm on medication for life to keep my blood thin.

But being able to educate the police, doctors, nurses and paramedics about what I've done is an honour. They always did their job, looked out for my best interests and saved my life. I am grateful.

Once I've done that, it sets me up right for the day and I can go out and be kind. And when I get home, no one is in my head, because I haven't harmed any one.

The kid who was unconscious for 37 years has finally woken up.

MY MISSION

Dear Reader

In all of my 23 years' experience of drugs and alcohol addiction along with the misery of jail, homelessness, massive amounts of crime, gang violence and behaviour, stabbings, mental health issues and self-harm, I never recall being made aware of the dangers of it all when I was young.

Maybe back then it was not really an issue like it is today, but the fact is that I still found it and it found me and so many others like me. Sadly some died. They didn't live to tell their story or warn kids about the life they didn't have.

I'm trying to change that. There was a missed opportunity many years ago for someone with experience to educate us when we were about 10, but it seems that the focus on academic development prevented any other life lessons.

But today we know full well that things are so much worse and getting worse all the time. It's so important that we are able to offer loving and caring support for all children and give them the life chances we can. We have to provide the education that helps them avoid making the choices I made so they can enjoy their childhood, their teenage years, their family life at Christmas and birthdays, and enjoy their friendships and relationships without ending up lonely and desperate in crack dens.

I've probably met well over 1000 addicts from all different backgrounds: male, female, white, black, Asian; from all religions and class backgrounds. Addiction does not discriminate. We have to educate everyone from the richest to the poorest.

Some primary and secondary schools book me year after year to educate their students. I think I've spoken to 400,000 young people from Year 4 to Year 13 (and some adults in rehab too) since I started this. My aim is to get to one million.

I hope this book has given you a sense of the dark world of addiction and also gives you the courage to try to help your kids, students, brothers and sisters to avoid it.

Best wishes

Paul

ACKNOWLEDGEMENTS

I'd like to thank Joanne, Ria's mum, for letting me see my daughter again and allowing me back into Ria's life. Also my mum for giving me life. The emergency services: the doctors who saved my life on so many occasions and who persevered in treating my injuries; the NHS nurses who made decisions and bent rules that in the end also helped me to get clean and sober; the paramedics who rescued me when I was dying; and to the police for doing their jobs and never giving up on me.

I'd also like to thank Mark who gave me the opportunity to write this book and Jordan for making it happen.